COLLECTOR'S GUIDE TO SOUVENIR PLATES

Arene Wiemers Burgess

77 Lower Valley Road, Atglen, PA 19310

Library of Congress Cataloging-in-Publication Data

Burgess, Arene Wiemers.
    Collector's guide to souvenir plates/Arene W. Burgess.
        p.   cm.
    Includes index.
    ISBN 0-7643-0099-7
    1. Souvenir plates--Collectors and collecting--United
States--Catalogs. 2. United States in art--Catalogs.
3. Potters--England--Catalogs. 4. Potters--United States--
Catalogs.
    I. Burgess, Arene Wiemers. Souvenir plates. II. Title.
III. Title: Souvenir plates
NK4695.P55B85   1996
738.309'42'075--dc20   96-20296
                                                            CIP

Printed in China
ISBN: 0-7643-0099-7
Book Design by Audrey L. Whiteside

Published by Schiffer Publishing Ltd.
77 Lower Valley Road
Atglen, PA 19310
Please write for a free catalog.
This book may be purchased from the publisher.
Please include $2.95 for shipping.
Try your bookstore first.

We are interested in hearing from authors
with book ideas on related subjects.

ACKNOWLEDGMENTS

I wish to express my thanks to all who helped in any way with the compilation of this book; first, to my husband, Chuck, who very patiently read copy, corrected typos and checked places and dates for accuracy. Also a special thanks to Dick and Noni Manley for their help with the Wedgwood section. Thanks also to friends who read the text to check for confusing and ambiguous statements.

CONTENTS

FOREWORD

In the early nineteen seventies when I began collecting souvenir plates, they were plentiful and inexpensive. Every antique shop had a few. Some appeared to be old and others did not (reproductions were not the problem — there weren't any!). There was no real information in the available books about American and English ceramics. The backstamps were more confusing than enlightening. Only the Wedgwood plates were dated. The articles in magazines such as *Hobbies* and *Spinning Wheel* filled in some of the gaps, but there was little reference to manufacturers or importers. Writers of the time were concerned with the views — not the makers.

If a collector were interested in Saratoga, New York, for example, how many different views could he expect to find? One could write to the manufacturers. But, most of them are no longer in business. Some have merged with other companies or moved. Records have been lost or destroyed. The only practical way to find out what had been made and what was available was to go through the collector magazines and read the ads. *Hobbies, Spinning Wheel, The Antiques Journal, The Antique Trader,* and a few others were checked beginning with January 1950. Nineteen fifty was chosen as the beginning year because there seemed to be no interest in souvenir plates before then. After going through nearly thirty years of these magazines, I had more than 3,000 note cards. Some, naturally, were duplicates.

Because more than ninety-five percent of all souvenir plates are marked (having been made since 1891 when it became mandatory for all imported items to be labeled) it seemed logical to list views by maker or importer. Each section is organized the same way. First appears the name of the company, its location, and dates of operation. A few paragraphs are devoted to the history and other pertinent data of the firm. In the list of views, the name (whenever possible the one given by the manufacturer or importer) is given first, then the border design and any unusual feature is mentioned. The color and size are last.

The lists are in no way complete. Wedgwood alone made more than 1,500 views. Rowland and Marsellus imported more than 400 different views. If one were to include items being made at the present time, the total would be mind boggling. There must be almost 4,000 different scenes of buildings, people, and historic sites and events, all made since 1880.

INTRODUCTION

It seems to be a trait of human nature that almost everyone who visits a place of historic interest or a strange city wants tangible evidence of having been there. Businessmen and hucksters are well aware of this as evidenced by the souvenirs sold at historic sites, festivals, parks, airports, etc.

Some souvenir plates were sold at the Centennial Exposition in Philadelphia in 1876. Even earlier, the Bennett Pottery of Baltimore had made a platter commemorating "Pickett's Charge." The oldest American souvenirs pictured in this book were imported by Wedgwood in the 1880s (views of the Old Man of the Mountain in New Hampshire).

The vogue of collecting and displaying souvenir plates really got under way in 1893 when the Jones, McDuffee, and Stratton Importing Company of Boston commissioned Wedgwood to make a series of blue plates with scenes of Boston and vicinity. The firm had previously given away calendar tiles with views on one side and was amazed at their popularity. By 1910, Jones, McDuffee, and Stratton had commissioned more than 300 different views. These plates were all the same color — dark rich blue — and had the same border, a wide band of full-blown roses. They resembled superficially the old Staffordshire ware which was even then being collected by antique enthusiasts of the time. Later, the company used different borders, a lighter shade of blue, and also other colors.

By 1910, at least a dozen potteries were making souvenir plates for various importers. Second only to Jones, McDuffee, and Stratton in scope of operation was the New York-based importing firm of Rowland and Marsellus. This firm began importing souvenir items about 1893 and was in business until the late 1930s.

After World War I, the advent of paved roads and affordable automobiles made traveling vacations feasible for middle class families. Patriotic and preservation groups were restoring and maintaining historic sites. The souvenir stand became an intrinsic part of almost every tourist attraction.

In the 1930s a commercially successful wire plate hanger came on the market, and collectors had a new and novel way to display their acquisitions. A new type of view also became popular - the college series. These were generally made in sets of six or twelve.

All of these plates, especially the earlier ones, are collectible. Many of the buildings and landmarks pictured no longer exist. Old city halls and courthouses, once the hub of almost every city of any size, are now centered in almost deserted downtowns. The architecturally-ornate libraries, train stations, schools and hospitals have been replaced by indistinguishable box-like structures.

Until recently, good contemporary plates were being made by firms such as Lenox, Spode, and Wedgwood. For every flower there is a weed. Many plates sold today at historic sites and tourist spots are coming from Japan. They are styled like the old ones. There are no backstamps — only a paper sticker, easily removed. A novice collector should probably buy only marked pieces although there are early unmarked examples.

THE POTTERS AND THEIR WARES

WILLIAM ADAMS and COMPANY

Tunstall Staffordshire, England
1789-

Adams is one of the oldest names in England's potting history. Geoffrey Godden lists thirty-five Adams marks in his comprehensive book, *Encyclopaedia of British Pottery and Porcelain Marks*. The firm of William Adams and Sons made souvenir items for the American market from about 1900 to 1965 when it affiliated with Wedgwood. When potteries merged, the production of souvenir items often ended because of cost constraints. The pottery could not or would not make less than a prescribed number which was often more than the market could absorb.

The John Roth Importing Company of Peoria, Illinois was Adams' chief distributor from the 1920s until 1965. The company's distinguishing mark is the word Jonroth or the initials J.H.R. and Co. The phrase "Old English Staffordshire Ware" is used with and without the Jonroth logo. Roth also used the firms of Ridgway, Royal Staffordshire, and others. For more information about the John Roth importing firm, see the Jonroth section.

Adena, Home of Thomas Worthington, after 1953, blue, 9 1/2 inches

Alaska-Yukon-Pacific Exposition, Seattle, 1909, center shows **Oriental ladies**, border is red and yellow feathers on a black and white background

Allentown, Pennsylvania, Soldiers' Monument, blue, 9 3/4 inches (see French, Mitchell, Woodbury)

America's Playground, Florida-Sunshine-flowers, center shows **Singing Tower**, twelve border scenes, (Jonroth) blue, 10 inches

Atlantic City, New Jersey, blue, 7 3/4 inches

Bangor, Maine, court house in center, flower border, blue, 10 1/2 inches

Barbara Fritchie's Home, Frederick, Maryland, blue

Bar Harbor, Maine, from Malden Hill, green, 10 inches

Baseball Hall of Fame, Cooperstown, Jonroth

Beatrice, Nebraska, six equal-sized views, public buildings, narrow border, c. 1915, blue, 8 inches

Beauvoir House, Jefferson Davis Shrine, camellia border, back has Confederate seal and flag, Jonroth, blue, 9 3/4 inches

Bellingrath Gardens, Mobile, Alabama, grotto in center, four border scenes, Jonroth, blue, 9 3/4 inches

Bermuda, Government House, marked 09, 1909? blue, 9 1/2 inches

Bermuda, Government House, same as above except has a black center scene

Boston Public Library, Adams and Son, blue

Boston State House, floral border, blue, 9 1/4 inches

Bruton Parrish Church, Williamsburg, Virginia, built 1710, Adams, blue, 10 inches; Jonroth, red, 10 inches

Bunker Hill Monument, about 1905, blue, pink, green, 9 1/2 inches

Bunker Hill Monument, Adams Souvenir Series, blue, 7 1/2 and 10 1/2 inches

Cape Cod, Massachusetts, Highland Light, blue, 7 1/2 inches

Capitol, Washington, D.C., floral border, blue

Capitol, Washington, D.C., Souvenir series, narrow floral border, 1929?

Cannon Memorial Chapel, University of Richmond, blue, 10 inches

Carlsbad Caverns, 9 inches

Citrus Tower, Clarmont, Florida, 6 3/4 inches

Cliff House, San Francisco, after 1936, 10 inches

Columbia, Missouri, (Picturesque) center is four columns on **University of Missouri** campus, blue, 10 inches

Columbus, Ohio, state capitol, floral border, blue, 10 inches

Coolidge Home, Plymouth, Vermont, floral border, (made for Ruth Aldrich Shop in Plymouth), blue, 6 and 10 inches, creamer and sugar, larger pitcher, cup and saucer, later reissues marked Jonroth

Crescent Hotel, Eureka Springs, Arkansas, floral border, blue, 10 1/2 inches

Congressional Library, Washington, D.C., blue, 10 1/2 inches

Custis-Lee Mansion, blue (see French, Mitchell, Woodbury)

Dells of the Wisconsin River, six views, narrow border, Jonroth, blue, 7 1/2 inches

Denver, Colorado, floral border, blue

Fairhaven, Connecticut, blue, 7 1/2 inches

Fall River Pass Store, Rocky Mountain National Park, blue, 5 inches

Faneuil Hall, Cradle of Liberty, Adams Souvenir Series, blue, green, 7 1/2 inches

Fenimore House, Cooperstown, N.Y., floral border, multi-color 9 3/4 inches

Fiftieth Anniversary, Gettysburg, 1863-1913, Lee, Meade, etc., blue, 7 1/2 inches

Florida state plate, blue, 9 1/2 inches

Flowing Well, (Titusville, Pennsylvania?) blue, 1905

Franciscan Monastery, Washington, D.C., blue, 5 inches

Franconia Notch, Old Man of the Mountain, blue, tile, 6 inches

General Lee and Staff, Battle of Gettysburg, 1863, blue, 10 1/2 inches

George Washington Masonic National Memorial, Alexandria, Virginia, blue, 10 inches

Gettysburg National Museum, Home of the Electrical Map, Jonroth, blue, 6 and 10 inches

Gettysburg, Pennsylvania, blue, 7 5/8 inches

Gettysburg, Pa., Eternal Light Peace Memorial, Jonroth, blue, 9 3/4 inches

Governor Langdon's Mansion, Portsmouth, New Hampshire, blue, 10 inches (see French, Mitchell, Woodbury)

Governor's Palace, Williamsburg, Virginia, four border scenes, Jonroth, blue, pink, 9 7/8 inches

Governor's Palace, Williamsburg, Virginia, roses border, Jonroth, bright blue, 10 inches

High Point Springs, Saratoga, New York, c. 1905, floral border, blue, 10 inches (see French, Mitchell, Woodbury)

Home of Daniel Webster, tea set, blue, 1925?

House of the Seven Gables, marked Adams, Tunstall, (backstamped Jones, McDuffee, and Stratton) blue, 9 inches

House of the Seven Gables, blue, pitcher, (Adams Souvenir Series)

Illinois Women's College, Jacksonville, Illinois, c. 1905, blue, 10 inches (see French, Mitchell, Woodbury)

Jackson Square, New Orleans, Louisiana, St. Louis Cathedral, Cabildo, State Historical Museum, narrow floral border, Jonroth, blue, 6 7/8 inches

Jamestown, Virginia, blue, 10 1/2 inches

Jamestown, Virginia, Old Church Tower, blue, 10 1/2 inches

K.S.A.C. (Kansas State Agricultural College), Manhattan, Kansas, blue, 7 1/4 inches

King's Chapel, Boston, blue, 10 inches

Landing of the Pilgrims, floral border, marked Warranted Staffordshire, blue

Lexington, Massachusetts, blue, 6 3/4 inches

Lincoln Head, 1909 Centenary, wreath around head, classical wreath border, white on blue, 7 1/2 inches

Lincoln Memorial, 10 inches

Lincoln's Birthplace, Hodgenville, Ky., log cabin center, four border scenes, Jonroth, blue, 6 and 10 inches

Lincoln's New Salem, Illinois, first Lincoln-Berry Store, five border scenes, Jonroth, blue, 9 3/4 inches, also pitcher, cup and saucer, blue

Longfellow's Wayside Inn, blue, 3 inches

Louisiana Purchase Exposition, Jefferson in center, sold at 1904 St. Louis World's Fair, blue, 10 inches

Mackinac Island, Michigan, floral border, deep blue, 10 inches

Marblehead, Massachusetts, Cradle of Liberty, center scene is of Ye Old Town House erected in 1737, blue, 10 inches

Mason City, Illinois, Centennial, 1957, new school in center, calendar border, Jonroth, 9 3/4 inches

Mayflower, gadroon border, blue 9 inches

Mayflower Arriving in Provincetown, Harbor, Nov. 11, 1620, dated 1901, deep blue, 7 1/2 inches

Mayflower II Crosses the Atlantic, May 1957, Jonroth, narrow floral border, blue, 7 inches

Monticello, five border scenes of estate, house in center, blue, 10 inches

Morse High School, Bath, Maine, 1903, blue, 10 inches (see French, Mitchell, Woodbury)

Moose Jaw Collegiate Institute, Saskatchewan, Canada, ashtray

Mount Vernon, blue, 7 1/2 and 10 inches; Jonroth, roses border, 7 1/2 and 10 inches; Jonroth, roses border, wine red, 10 inches

Naugatuck, Connecticut, blue, 6 3/4 inches

Niagara Falls, New York, blue, 6 3/4 inches; platter, 11 by 16 inches

Nottingham, Massachusetts, 1933, blue, 10 inches

Norwalk, Ohio, blue, 9 inches

Old Faithful Geyser, geyser in center, four park scenes in border, Jonroth, soft blue, 10 inches (marked '39—date?)

Old Church tower, Jamestown, Virginia, blue, 1957

Old Man of the Mountain, New Hampshire, blue, 9 inches

Old Mill at Nantucket, blue, 10 inches

Old New York

Old Oaken Bucket, 1903 blue, 10 inches (see French, Mitchell, Woodbury)

Old Scituate Light, Home of Rebecca and Abigail Bates, Heroines of the War of 1812, blue, 10 1/2 inches

Old State House, Boston, marked Tunstall, blue, 7 1/2 inches

Old Stone Mill, Newport, Rhode Island, floral border, dark blue, 10 1/4 inches

Oldest House on Nantucket, 7 inches

Orleans, Massachusetts, six scenes, blue

Park Street Church, Boston, floral border

Patriotic Ware, dinner set between 1914 and 1940, yellow and red border with stylized American eagle in center

Patriotic Ware, various states coats of arms

Pilgrim Memorial Monument, Provincetown, Massachusetts, tile, blue, 6 inches

Pipe Organ, the, Hiwig Caverns, New York, 1842, roses border, bright blue, 10 inches (a late example but not marked Jonroth)

Plymouth Rock, flowers and vases border, blue, 10 inches

Portland, Maine, blue, 7 3/4 inches

Portrait and Original Home of Daniel Webster, Marshfield, Massachusetts, Adams Souvenir Series tea set about 1925, blue

Priscilla and John Alden, "Why Don't You Speak for Yourself, John?" Jonroth, floral border, blue, 10 inches

Provincetown, Massachusetts, platter, floral border, deep blue, 9 3/4 by 11 3/4 inches

Provincetown, Massachusetts, views of, Adams Souvenir Series, blue, 7 1/2 inches

Provincetown Railway Wharf and Harbor, Adams and Son mark, blue

Public Library, Boston, 7 1/2, 9, and 10 inches (smallest one has eagle backstamp)

Robin's Nest, tile, West Thorn, White Mountains, New Hampshire

Royal Gorge, Colorado, view on one side only, pitcher, blue, 2 3/4 inches

St. Augustine, Florida, (imported by W.H. Dubois) colorful border, 12 inches

St. Louis World's Fair, 1904, Palace of Electricity; Palace of Liberal Arts; Palace of Machinery; Palace of Varied Industries; (possibly part of a set of six) pink, blue, all 9 3/4 inches

St. Paul's School, blue

St. Petersburg, narrow border, six scenes, blue-grey

Salem Witch, Salem in 1692, blue, (Wm. Adams)

Salt Lake City, Temple. Jonroth, blue

Schenectady, New York, Oldest House in Town, (Old Dutch Colonial), Governor Yates House, blue, 7 1/2 inches

Spanish Arms, St. Augustine, Florida, Etruscan Ware, dull black, gold edge, 8 1/2 inches

South Hampton, Long Island, blue, 7 3/4 inches

Stand Rock, Picturesque, Wisconsin Dells, roses border, Jonroth, blue, 10 inches

State House, Boston, blue, 10 inches

Stewart-Haskins Free Library, 1904, blue, 9 3/4 inches (see French, Mitchell, Woodbury)

Summit House, Pike's Peak, blue, 10 1/4 inches

Temple Square, Salt Lake City, pitcher, blue, 4 inches

Temples of Latter Day Saints, The Temple, Salt Lake City, center, seven temples in border, (one is territory of Hawaii-pre-1959) bright blue, 10 inches; creamer, Jonroth

Toledo, Ohio, eagle, thirteen stars, 9 inches

Townsend, Massachusetts, 1932, blue, 10 inches

Turkey Run State Park, The Inn, blue, 10 inches

U.S. Capitol Building, Washington, D.C., floral border, Jonroth, 7 5/8 inches

U.S. Capitol Building, c. 1910, floral border, bright blue, 10 1/2 inches

U.S. Capitol, Washington, D.C., Adams Souvenir Series, blue, 9 inches

United States Congressional Library, Adams Souvenir Series, blue, 9 inches

University of Illinois, Main Hall, Urbana, Illinois, four border scenes, blue, 9 inches

Utah, Temple Square, backstamped Zion Co-operative Mercantile Institute, Salt Lake City, multi-colored, 10 inches

Vassar College

Vicksburg Courthouse, Vicksburg, Mississippi, camellia border, Jonroth, blue, 10 inches

Washington, D.C.

Washington Monument, floral border, blue

Washington's Headquarters, Morristown, New Jersey, blue, 9 inches

Washington's headquarters, Valley Forge, cup and sauce, blue, 1960s

Webster Court House, Plymouth, New Hampshire, where Daniel Webster Made his First Plea in 1806, blue, 7 3/4 inches

White House, blue, 10 1/2 inches

William and Mary College, Wren Building, Jonroth, blue, 9 3/4 inches

Williamsburg, Virginia, Bruton Parish Church, blue, 10 inches

Wisconsin Dells, handpainted with blue border

World's Fair, New York, 1939, set of six service plates, marked Tiffany, blue

Yankee Doodle, Spirit of '76, floral swag border, blue, 10 1/2 inches (see French, Mitchell, Woodbury)

Yarmouth, Nova Scotia, blue, 7 1/4 inches

BAWO and DOTTER
Importers
New York 1864-1910

The importing firm of Bawo and Dotter was founded in 1864 in New York by Francis M. Bawo and Charles T. Dotter. For many years the firm imported china from France and Germany, even setting up its own factories in these countries at various times. At the turn of the century, B. and D. was importing and distributing souvenir and commemorative plates from England. The suppliers were Spode, Ridgway, Goss, and others. Evidently this company did not import souvenir plates very extensively. The firm probably took orders for groups like the D.A.R. A distinguishing feature is the use of color overlay with blue or green. Rowland and Marsellus also used this on a few pieces but did not continue the practice after about 1910.

Battle of Germantown, Attack on Jude Chew's House, fruit and flower border, 10 inches
Battle of Lake Erie, fruit and flower border, blue with color overlay, 10 inches
Bunker Hill Monument, Charlestown, Massachusetts, fruit and flower border, 10 inches
Capitol, Washington, D.C., fruit and flower border, blue, 10 inches
Commodore John Paul Jones, fruit and flower border, blue, 10 inches
Daytona, Florida, The Big Tree, rolled edge, blue, 10 inches
Death of Captain Lawrence, fruit and flower border, blue, 10 inches
DeSoto's Discovery of the Mississippi 1541, fruit and flower border, blue, 10 inches
Faneuil Hall, Boston, from the Harbor, fruit and flower border, blue, 10 inches
Federal Hall, Wall Street, fruit and flower border, blue with color overlay, 9 3/4 inches
Independence Hall, fruit and flower border, green with color overlay, 9 3/4 inches
Jacksonville, Florida, rolled edge, blue, 10 inches
Landing of Roger Williams, fruit and flower border, blue, 10 inches
Miami, Florida, rolled edge, blue, 10 inches

Molly Pitcher, Battle of Monmouth, fruit and flower border, blue, (brown), 10 inches
Niagara Falls, blue, 10 inches
Old City Gates, St. Augustine, Florida, fruit and flower border, deep blue, 10 inches
Patrick Henry Addressing the Virginia Assembly, fruit and flower border, blue, 10 inches
St. Augustine, Florida, blue, 10 inches
Washington Crossing the Delaware, December 25, 1776, fruit and flower border, blue, 10 inches
Whirlpool Rapids, Niagara Falls, fruit and flower border, green with color overlay, 10 inches
William Penn's Treaty with the Indians, fruit and flower border, blue, 10 inches

FRANK BEARDMORE and COMPANY
Fenton Staffordshire, England
1904-1913

This short-lived firm specialized in the production of souvenir plates for the American and Canadian markets as evidenced by the great number still available. Most of the views are of buildings or popular tourist spots of the day. The company made innumerable small plates, and larger ones too, with six or seven equal-sized views separated by scrolls and flowers. Some of the larger plates have a distinctive stylized border such as the "tulips" on the Washington Monument plate. The small plates were sometimes made in a coupe shape (a concave shape with no foot, rim, or border) which gives them a curiously modern appearance. Like many of their contemporaries, Beardmore used the rolled edge, a fad of the time throughout Beardmore's years of production (see Rowland Marsellus). There is also great variety in the shades of blue, ranging from dull slate gray to bright royal or greenish-blue. About half the plates are dated with an incised number. The backstamps are: Beardmore, Frank Beardmore and Co., or a circle with a dove holding an olive branch in its beak.

Alamo, the, built in 1718, no border, 1907, slate blue, 7 1/2 inches

American College Plate, The Pen is Mightier than the Sword, bright blue, 10 inches

Bellefontaine, Pennsylvania, blue, 7 1/2 inches

Boston, Massachusetts, five scenes of equal size, slate blue, 7 3/4 inches

Boston, leaf border, six scenes, slate blue, 9 1/2 inches

Canton, Illinois, six scenes, slate blue, 7 3/4 inches

Capitol, Washington, D.C., no border, imported by George Bowman and Co., blue-green, 7 1/2 inches

Capitol, Washington, brown, 9 and 10 inches; blue, 9 and 10 inches; brown with green border, 9 inches

Coats of Arms of Thirteen Colonies, United States as of 1776

Columbus, Ohio, state capitol, blue, 7 1/2 inches

Congressional Library, brown, 9 and 10 inches

Dartmouth College

Decatur, Illinois, seven scenes, slate blue, 7 3/4 inches

Denver, Colorado, capitol in center, six equal-sized scenes, wide rolled edge, slate blue, 10 inches

Earlham College, Richmond, Indiana

Fall River Line, four ships, slate blue, 8 inches

Grand Forks, North Dakota, blue, 10 inches

Heart Island (1,000 Islands) floral border, dark slate blue, 9 inches

Indianapolis, Indiana

Independence Hall, no border, coupe shape, slate blue, 7 1/2 inches

Kenton, Ohio, blue, 7 inches

Kingston, New York

Minneapolis, Minnesota, state capitol, blue, 7 1/2 inches

Lincoln, Nebraska, state capitol, blue, 7 1/2 inches

Lincoln High School, Seattle, Washington, blue, 7 inches

Minnehaha Falls, Minneapolis, Minnesota, blue, 7 inches

Miles Standish House, borderless style, blue, 7 inches

National Emblem, series of plates of Europe and U.S., green and yellow borders with red, 10 inches

U.S.
Italy
Austria-Hungary
Sweden
Netherlands
Spain
Portugal
France
others?

New Haven, Connecticut, six scenes, leaf border, slate blue, 9 inches

Newport, Rhode Island, five scenes, slate blue, 7 1/4 inches

Niagara, souvenir of, center is Prospect Point, top of border crossed American and Canadian flags, six scenes in border, rolled edge, slate blue, 10 inches

Old State House, Boston, blue, 9 inches

Parliament Building, Fredericton, New Brunswick, narrow leaf border, slate blue, 7 1/2 inches

Prospect Point, American and Canadian Falls, stylized border, slate blue, 10 inches

Quebec, center scene of bluff, six border scenes, rolled edge

Rockaway Beach, New York, six equal-sized views with stylized tulip border, narrow rolled edge, slate blue, 9 inches

Salt Lake City, Utah, tumbler, blue, 3 5/8 inches

St. John, New Brunswick, leaf border, blue, 9 inches

St. Paul, Minnesota, 7 1/2 inches

Stag Island, Marysvale, Michigan, narrow border, blue

Superior, Wisconsin, souvenir of, five scenes, leaf border, slate blue, 9 1/2 inches

Tampa, Florida, five border scenes, blue, 7 3/4 inches

Toledo, Ohio, Public Library, stylized border, slate blue, 10 inches

United States Congressional Library, blue, 7 3/4 inches

Washington Monument, Washington, D.C., stylized border rolled edge, imported by Bowman, deep bright blue, 10 inches

Washington Monument, Richmond, Virginia, no border, slate blue, 7 3/4 inches

Washington's Headquarters, Newburgh, New York, rolled edge, tulip border, slate blue, 9 1/4 inches

Winona, Minnesota, five views, slate blue, 7 3/4 inches

Worcester, Massachusetts, New Railroad Station, no border, slate blue, 7 3/4 inches

York, Maine, grey, 10 inches

BEDFORD WORKS
(RIDGWAY'S LIMITED)
Sheldon, Hanley Staffordshire, England
1920-1952

This firm became a subsidiary of the Ridgway Potteries in 1952. Bedford made souvenir items for Jonroth (probably in the post-World War era only, as none of the examples found appear to be from the twenties or thirties). Many of Bedford's plates appear identical to those made by Adams.

Cabildo, the, Old Spanish Court Building, New Orleans, Louisiana, roses border, light blue, 10 1/4 inches

Grand Canyon National Park, Arizona, roses border, medium blue, 10 1/4 inches

Historic Warren County Courthouse, Vicksburg, Mississippi, roses border, bright blue, 10 1/4 inches

Hot Springs, Arkansas, blue, 10 inches

Longfellow's Home, cup and saucer, roses border, pink

Lorado Taft Alma Mater, University of Illinois, statue in center, narrow band of roses border, pink, 7 inches

MacMurray College, Jacksonville, Illinois, four border scenes of Illinois state institutions, center view is main hall of MacMurray, blue, 10 1/4 inches

Mt. Le Conte, Great Smokey Mountains National Park, floral border, blue, lavender, 10 inches

Natural Bridge of Virginia, tile, light blue, 6 inches

Salt Lake City, cup and saucer, blue

Starved Rock State Park, on the Illinois River, four border scenes of park attractions, blue, 10 1/4 inches

EDWIN BENNETT POTTERY COMPANY
Baltimore, Maryland
1890-

This company was organized from the earlier Bennett Potteries which originated in Baltimore, Maryland. The Bennett name is most commonly associated with the Rebecca-at-the-Well teapot and other brown glazed ware. The company also made yellow ware, granite ware, stone china, cream colored ware, and semi-porcelain. From 1890 on the firm used the motto Bono Fame est Melior Zona Aurea. The motto encircles the globe with a sword piercing through. The name of the pottery does not generally appear with this mark. The only commemorative found was a blue plate of Washington, D.C. Undoubtedly others were made.

A.C. BOSSELMAN and COMPANY
Importers
New York
1904-1930

The Bosselman Company imported souvenir plates made by Ridgway. Most, but not all, have the rolled edge associated with Rowland and Marsellus. The colors are generally a clear, bright blue. Either the company was not into the blue plate field very extensively, or much was unmarked. The Bosselman mark is not common even in large collections.

Indianapolis, Indiana, Soldiers and Sailors Monument

Landing of Hendrick Hudson, marked Boffelman, misprint for Bosselman? also marked R and M

Milwaukee, Wisconsin, City Hall

New York, Statue of Liberty

Plymouth, Massachusetts, Landing of the Pilgrims

Valley Forge, Pennsylvania, Washington's Headquarters

GEORGE H. BOWMAN and COMPANY
Importers
New York and Cleveland
1888-1930

The Bowman mark will be found on plates made by Doulton, Beardmore and others. Like many another companies, Bowman boasted of being "sole importers," and like many another, seems to have been the victim of the Depression and changing tastes.

Capitol, Washington, D.C., blue, 9 inches
Penn's Treaty with the Indians, fruit and flower border, blue, 10 inches
United States Capitol, blue, 10 inches

SAMPSON BRIDGWOOD and SON, Ltd., ANCHOR POTTERY
Longton Staffordshire, England
1804-

This old firm evidently did not make many commemoratives, as can be seen from the short list below.

Administration Building, Columbian Exposition, 1893, brown, 8 inches
Crawford Cooking Ranges (made for Walker, Pratt, Boston,Mass.), blue, photo in Rowland and Marsellus section
Hall of Mines, World's Fair, 1893, rose border, black center, square, 6 3/4 inches
Transportation Building, Columbian Exposition, 1893, brown, 8 inches

BRITISH ANCHOR POTTERY COMPANY, Ltd.
Longton Staffordshire, England
1884-

Trying to date the products of this company is somewhat difficult as the company reissued views at various times. Some of the reissues appear at first glance to be older than the originals. British Anchor probably began making plates for the American market about 1910 or a little later. The company was still making them in the 1960s when the color line had expanded to include pink and mauve. The firm may have been represented in its early years by Rowland and Marsellus since most early plates have the fruit and flower border or the rolled edge. One se-ries was called "Ye Old Historical Pottery." At least part of the series was numbered, although none seems to have been dated. The pottery was closed between 1940 and 1945 and resumed operations after World War II. See Rowland and Marsellus for listing of Ye Olde Historical Pottery plates.

Battle of Bunker Hill, June 17, 1776, fruit and flower border, backstamped Ye Old Historical Pottery, post-1945, deep blue, 10 inches
Boston Massacre and Old State House, fruit and flower border, blue, 10 inches
Biddeford, Maine, March 1913, deep blue
Capitol at Washington, D.C., capitol building in center, four border scenes, deep blue, 9 inches
Faneuil Hall from the Harbor, Boston, fruit and flower border, deep blue, 10 inches (same backstamp as first example)
Faneuil Hall, hall in center, four border scenes of Boston including John Hancock House, backstamped no. 1, Ye Olde Historical Pottery, reg. no. 533308, bright blue, 9 inches
Gloucester, Massachusetts, 1913?
Mt. Vernon, George and Martha Washington in medallion at top, blue, 10 inches
National Monument to the Forefathers, fruit and flower border, deep blue, 10 inches
Natural Bridge of Virginia, cup and saucer, pink
Newport, Rhode Island, blue, 9 inches
Patrick Henry Addressing the Virginia Assembly, Ye Olde Historical Pottery, no. 1, pink
Perry's Victory on Lake Erie, center scene of Perry in boat, four border scenes, white della robbia band one inch wide around edge, backstamped Ye Old Historical Pottery, no. 4, reg. no. 563726, bright blue, 10 inches
Pilgrims, Plymouth, creamer, pink, 1960s
Put-in-Bay, Ohio, cup and saucer, green, early example
Richmond, Virginia, souvenir of, center scene of city hall, six border scenes, rolled edge, pre-1940, bright blue, 10 inches
San Francisco, views of, center is Golden Gate Inlet by Moonlight, six border scenes, deep, almost flowed blue, 10 inches
Snowball Dining Room in Mammoth Cave, Kentucky, fruit and flower border, backstamped Jonroth, dark blue, 10 inches
Washington Crossing the Delaware, backstamped no. 9 Ye Olde Historical Pottery
Washington's Prayer at Valley Forge, fruit and flower border, blue, mauve, possibly pink (1960s), 10 inches

17

BUFFALO POTTERY
Buffalo, New York
1901

Elbert Hubbard, founder of the Roycrofters arts and crafts movement based in East Aurora, New York, was directly responsible for the establishment of the Buffalo Pottery Company. He and his brother-in-law, John Larkin, were partners in a soap manufacturing business. Hubbard conceived the idea of by-passing the middleman and selling directly to the consumer. As an added incentive, the Larkin Company offered premiums with the cleaning products. This idea proved to be so successful Hubbard thought they ought to make their own premiums too, thereby passing up the middleman again. The Buffalo Pottery was established in 1901 and almost immediately had nine kilns operating. Commemoratives were just a small part of the total output. Probably the most collected "Buffalo" today is Deldare. Practically all the commemoratives were made between 1905 and 1911. Since 1930, the company has made only hotel and restaurant ware. A detailed history of the company can be found in any of several books about twentieth century American potteries.

Bangor, Maine
Biltmore Hotel
Eads Bridge, St. Louis, Missouri, souvenir of, scalloped edge, floral border, blue, 10 1/2 inches
Erie Canal, lacy border, black
Faneuil Hall, green, 10 and 10 1/2 inches; black, 10 inches; blue-green, 10 1/4 inches; blue, 10 and 10 1/2 inches; multi-color, 7 1/4 inches
Federal Building, Helena, Montana, 1909, 7 1/4 inches
George Washington, pitcher, helmet shape, 1907, blue and gold, 7 1/4 inches
George Washington plate for the C. and C. Railroad, 11 inches
Grand Review of the Army of the Potomac by President Lincoln at Falmouth, Virginia, April 1863, platter, blue, 11 by 14 inches
Hamilton College, green

Here died Volk Victorious Tercentenary. 1759, Quebec Monument, border is 10 flags of provinces, seal at top, 7 1/4 inches
Home of Emma Willard, tea set for the Women's Christian Temperance Union
Independence Hall, blue, 10 and 10 1/4 inches; blue-green, 10 1/4 inches
Jack Knife Bridge, Buffalo, New York, 7 1/4 inches
John Paul Jones, pitcher, 1907, blue on cream, 10 inches
Lafayette Square, Buffalo, New York, blue-green, 6 1/2 inches
Landing of Roger Williams, pitcher, 1907
Locks, the, Lockport, New York, "Old Home Week" 1910, green, 7 1/2 inches
Miles Standish, pitcher, nine scenes, 9 inches
Modern Woodmen of America, 1911
Mt. Vernon, floral border, blue, 10 inches; blue-green, 10 inches, green, 10 inches; multi-color, 7 1/2 inches
New Bedford commemorative, jug, sepia
New Bedford, blue, 10 1/2 inches
New Orleans, creamer
New York Central Steam Engine, 1837 emblem on floral border, dish, 5 1/2 by 8 1/2 inches
Niagara Falls, floral border, green, 10 and 10 1/4 inches; blue, 10 inches; green, plain border, 6 1/2 inches
St. Mary Magdalen Church, 6 1/4 inches
Statue of Liberty, 7 1/4 inches
Terminal Building, 7 1/2 inches
Trinity Church, 7 1/2 inches
U.S. Capitol, blue, 10 and 10 1/4 inches; blue-green, 7 1/2 and 10 1/2 inches; green, 10 and 10 1/4 inches
Wannemaker Store, 1861-1911, Jubilee Year, 4 3/4 inches
White House, black, 10 inches; blue, 10 and 10 1/2 inches; blue-green, 10 1/2 inches; multi-color ?
Woodmen of the World, green

CARR CHINA COMPANY
Grafton, West Virginia
1916-1952

The Carr China Company made a very fine grade of vitrified china, chiefly for hotels and restaurants. The firm also made many commemorative items for groups like the Masons, the Eastern Star, 4-H, fraternities, and other organizations. Carr made dinnerware for the United States Military Academy, the United States Naval Academy, the United States Quartermaster's Corps, and the State Conservation Commission summer camps. The name Carr is mentioned quite prominently in Barber's and other books about American potteries. James Carr (1820-1900), a native of England, established the New York City Pottery in 1863. This firm was in business for nearly thirty-five years and received many honors, some of which are listed in Barber. James' son came to Wheeling, West Virginia in 1891 and was associated with the Warwick China Company, eventually becoming president of the firm. In 1917, Thomas Carr, supposedly having retired from Warwick, came to Grafton to assist with the new pottery being formed. He was one of the principal founders of the Carr China Company. Thomas's son-in-law, Wheeler Carr Bachman, served as president of the firm until his death in 1932; his widow took over until her son, Wheeler Carr Backman II, became president in 1949. The company went out of business in 1952 and the factory burned in 1962.

Antoine's of New Orleans, Red Devil, cup and saucer

California Mission Inn dinnerware

Mother's Day, word "Mother" on front, bouquet of roses, various colored borders

Monticello, Home of Thomas Jefferson, ash tray

Old Covered Bridge of Philippi, West Virginia (scene of first land battle of Civil War, 1862-1952), probably last commemorative made by Carr

St. Andrew's Methodist Church, Mother's Day plate, back has history of Anna Jarvis who founded Mother's Day (the first service was held at Grafton on May 12, 1907)

Tygart River Reservoir Dam, blue, green, black, 8 inches

CAULDON, Ltd.
Hanley Staffordshire, England
1905-1962

The Cauldon Pottery was founded in 1774 at Stoke-on-Trent and was sold to Pountney and Company in 1962. The following is a brief history drawn from a letter from an official of the company:

"For many years the Cauldon Pottery made fine china. The company became Royal Cauldon in the late 1880s when Queen Victoria visited the factory to choose a pattern for one of the Royal households. (This pattern, still in production, is called Victoria.) In 1962 Royal Cauldon was purchased by Pountney and Company and production was moved to Bristol. Only earthenware was made there. In 1969 the factory at Bristol was closed when the site was sold. A new factory was built in Redruth, Cornwall. Two years later, Pountney went bankrupt. In January 1975 the company became Cauldon Bristol Potteries Cornwell, Ltd., owned by A.G. Richardson and Company, Ltd., founded in 1915. Before going into bankruptcy, Pountney had sold everything, including old pattern books, copper plates, and engravings for printing. Evidently Cauldon did not produce souvenirs for the popular market, as the few items found seem to have been made for special occasions."

Abraham Lincoln, bulbous pitcher, Lincoln portrait on two sides and printed below "With malice toward none, with charity for all," blue

Admiral George Dewey, backstamped "souvenir of the dinner given for Admiral and Mrs. Dewey by the Union League Club of Brooklyn, February 8, 1990," blue, 10 1/2 inches

Chicago, Illinois, set of six different historical scenes, made for Carson, Pirie, Scott and Co., blue, gadroon edge

Perry Transferring his Colors, blue, 10 1/2 inches

Revolutionary series, two plaques, Washington and Lafayette at Valley Forge; Yankee Doodle or Spirit of '76, blue, 16 and 18 inches

COALPORT
Stoke-on-Trent
(since 1926) Staffordshire, England

This venerable firm, which began operations in 1795, did not make many commemoratives. The two listed are probably porcelain.

Admiral Dewey, Manilla Bay, May 1898, Dewey is center, six ships in border, gold edge, pale blue, 10 1/2 inches

Santiago, Schley in center, July 1898, blue, 10 1/2 inches

COLONIAL POTTERY

see F. Winkle and Company

W.T. COPELAND and SONS, Ltd.
SPODE WORKS
Stoke, Staffordshire, England
1847-

Next to Wedgwood, Spode is probably "the" name most people associate with fine English porcelain and earthenware. The formation and dissolution of partnerships throughout the nineteenth century is more than a little confusing. Before 1833 the company was Spode; between 1833 and 1847 it was Copeland and Garrett; in 1875 Spode was added to the backstamp. After 1890 it was Spode, Copeland's China, England. The word Spode has been part of its backstamp ever since.

Beginning in 1888 impressed date marks have been used. The code is shown in Godden's *Encyclopaedia of Marks*. For example, Y 92 means July 1892. Since the 1930s this company has made hundreds of views of colleges, universities, and cities. These are generally sets of twelve. Many, but not all, of the plates have a distinctive gadroon rim which was also a feature of Copeland and Garrett's earthenware. The gadroon rim is a white, narrow, scalloped, rope-like edge (see photo of Buffalo Bill plate). Many other potteries, including at least one American firm, copied this style of border. Sets or series made in the 1950s are more often found in black than blue.

Annapolis scenes

Bar Harbor, Acadia National Park, published by F.L. Sherman, Bar Harbor, Maine, gadroon border, black, 10 3/4 inches (part of a set, others are Thunder Hole, Views from Cadillac Mountain, etc.)

Boston, R. H. Sterns Centennial, black, 10 1/4 inches
> King's Chapel
> Old State House
> Boston Commons
> Old North Church
> Public Gardens
> others?

Buffalo Bill 1846-1946 (portrait) memorialized at Cody, Wyoming, his home, by Gertrude Vanderbilt Whitney statue and Buffalo Bill Museum, gadroon edge, brown, 10 3/4 inches

Chicago, University of, set of 12, black on cream, 10 1/2 inches, 1931
> Cobb Hall
> Hall Court
> Hitchcock Hall
> Billings Memorial Hospital
> Hutchinson Court
> Mitchell Hall
> Harper Court
> (others)

Columbian Exposition, 1893, stone china coffee pot, pitcher, 8 inches, tankard shape, Columbus and his Men, ivory on blue background

Centennial Hall, flower border, blue, 10 inches (made for Caldwell)

Constitution Hall, flower border, blue, 10 inches

Emporia, Kansas, centennial, 1857-1957, gadroon border

John Alden and Priscilla, blue, 10 1/2 inches

Kansas City, Missouri, city hall and courthouse, black, 10 1/2 inches

King Edward's Hotel, Toronto, Canada, blue, 10 1/2 inches

King's Chapel, Boston, floral border, blue, 10 1/2 inches

Longfellow's Library, Cambridge, Mass., floral border, blue, 10 1/4 inches

Mall, the, Boston Common, 6 inches

Mayflower in Plymouth Harbor, pitcher, 1897

Mayflower and Plymouth Plantation Arms, deep blue, 5 1/2 inches

New York World's Fair, 1939, for Abraham and Strauss, Brooklyn, 1st edition, set of six, deep blue, 10 1/2 inches
> Food Building
> Shelter Building
> Textile Building
> Hall of Communications
> ?
> ?

Orphan Asylum, City of Brooklyn, 75th Anniversary, 1908, deep blue, 10 inches

Pilgrim Commemorative, cup and saucer, large, blue with gold trim, Tiffany

Portland, Maine, Longfellow's Home, blue

St. Louis, Missouri, historical scenes, set of 12, 1950, gadroon edge, black, 10 1/2 inches (some were reissued in the early 1970s)
  - Eads Bridge
  - Old Cathedral
  - Old Courthouse
  - The Robert E. Lee (steamboat)
  - Veiled Prophet Parade
  - Chouteau Mansion
  - 2nd Street Presbyterian Church
  - Race Track at Old St. Louis Fairgrounds
  - Mississippi River
  - Jefferson Barracks
  - Louisiana Purchase Exposition (St. Louis World's Fair)
  - First Railroad West of the Mississippi

Springfield, Massachusetts, tercentenary, 1686-1936, blue, 10 1/2 inches

Stanford University, the Arcade and the Library, part of a set?, black, 10 inches

Why Don't You Speak for Yourself, John?, blue, 9 inches

CROWN DUCAL
A.G. Richardson and Co., Ltd.
Tunstall Staffordshire, England
1916-1975

Crown Ducal was a trademark and backstamp used by the A.G. Richardson Company from 1916 until 1933 or 1934 for decorated earthenware. The Crown Ducal factory was sold in 1975 (letter from A. G. Richardson and Co., Ltd.) The company made many commemorative plates in blue, pink, lavender, green, and brown, as well as a complete dinner set in blue (also pink) called **Colonial Times**. This set showed various early American heroes, places, and events and was made in 1932 (possibly 1933) to take advantage of the 1932 Washington Birthday Bicentennial. Most of the Crown Ducal commemoratives were made in the late 1920s and early 1930s.

Catalina Island, pale blue

Charlestown, South Carolina, powder magazine in center, four border scenes, pink, 10 inches (has cut corners giving it a rectangular shape

Colonial Times, dinner set, pink and blue, plates, 10 inches
  - When the First President Gave Thanks
  - First Thanksgiving in America
  - Monticello
  - Mayflower in Plymouth Harbor
  - Independence Hall
  - Signing the Contract on the Mayflower
  - Mt. Vernon
  - Landing of the Pilgrims
  - Marriage of Pocahontas plates 9 inches
  - First Thanksgiving in America plates 9 inches, square
    - Marriage of Pocahontas
    - Landing of the Pilgrims
    - Independence Hall
    - Penn's Treaty with the Indians
    - Going to Church
    - When the First President Gave Thanks
  - Yankee Doodle soups 8 inches
  - Paul Revere's Ride plates 7 inches
  - Speak for Yourself, John plates 6 inches

  Watching the Battle of Bunker Hill cups and saucers, cup is Plymouth Rock and the Mayflower, saucer is Pilgrim maiden at flax wheel

This is only a partial list. There are platters, bowls, teapot, sugar and creamer, etc.

George Washington Bicentennial Memorial plates, square; green, lavender, blue, pink, 1932, set of 12 shows events in the life of Washington, 8 1/2 inches

George Washington Bicentennial Memorial plates, round, blue, 10 1/2 inches (same views as set above)

John Adams Proposing Washington for Commander-in-Chief of American Army, blue, lavender, 10 inches

Lafayette at Mt. Vernon, 1732-1932

Monticello, blue, 10 1/2 inches

Old New Orleans, scenes for Coleman S. Adler and Sons. Inc., Jewelers, New Orleans, set of six, stylized scroll border, blue, 10 inches
  - Brulatour Courtyard, Typical of Vieux Carre
  - Lacy Iron Grillwork, St. Peter and Royal Streets
  - St. Louis Cathedral and Cabildo facing Jackson Square Jackson Square Walled Garden
  - Madam Jumel's Legacy
  - Pirate's Alley

Old New Orleans, same views as above except with cobalt and gold border, 10 inches (porcelain)

Spirit of '76, made for Stern's, blue, 10 inches

21

Washington Commemoratives, della robbia border, multi-color and blue, 10 inches
  Washington at Trenton
  Washington's Birthplace
  Washington Crossing the Delaware, 10 1/2 inches

DAVENPORT
Longport Staffordshire, England
1793-1897

The mark Davenport's Ltd. appears on the back of the blue plates pictured. This mark was used from 1881-1887 which would indicate that souvenir plates were being made and imported sooner than has been generally assumed. According to Godden, this mark was used from 1881 to 1887 — but Union Station was not completed until 1894.

Detroit City Hall, blue
Fort Wayne, Indiana, Allen County Courthouse, blue, 10 inches
Grand Rapids, Michigan, Winegar's Furniture Store, blue, 10 inches
Kansas State Capitol, blue, 10 inches
St. Louis views (all are blue)
  Compton Hill Water Tower
  The Eads Bridge
  St. Louis University and St. Xavier's Church
  Union Station, St. Louis

(ROYAL) DOULTON
Doulton and Company, Ltd. 1972
Burslem, Staffordshire, England
1882

Although known primarily for figurines and other decorative objects, the Royal Doulton firm was actively engaged in making blue and other color commemorative plates for some time, from about 1900 until the late 1920s. Doulton is now a part of the Allied English Potteries and is known as Royal Doulton Tableware, Ltd. The Doulton company made the famous Gibson Girl plates. There were twenty-four in the set. In the center of each (in black transfer) is a scene in the life of a beautiful young widow. The border is a stylized design in blue. These came out in 1900-1901.

Aero Plane, Hudson-Fulton Celebration, 1909, 10 1/2 inches
American tom turkey with 5 hens, (date 1-01), probably part of a set with a platter, blue, 10 inches
Balanced Rock, Niagara Falls, deep blue, 10 inches
Banff National Park, 5 scenes, 10 inches
Birthplace of John Whittier, blue, 9 1/2 inches
Bermuda, center scene is Sir George Summers wrecked on the island 1609, border scenes of Bermuda, coupe shape, bright blue, 10 inches
Capitol, Washington, D.C., imported by Bowman, blue, 10 inches
Congressional Library, imported by Bowman, blue, 10 inches (two versions, different borders)
Cornell University, portrait of Ezra Cornell in center, 1952, light blue, 10 inches
Duchess County, New York Society, set of six, blue, 10 inches
  The Collegiate College
  Meiser Home, Weppinger Falls
  ?
Genesee River, two inch dahlia and leaf border, backstamped 14th dinner Genesee Society, blue, 10 1/2 inches
George Washington portrait, black on mustard, 10 1/2 inches
George Washington portrait, imported by Bowman, blue, 10 inches
George Washington Marching on Trenton, Christmas 1776, dated 1905, deep blue, 10 1/2 inches
Gibson Girls, set of 24, semi-porcelain, black centers, blue borders, 1900-1901, 10 1/2 inches, series is called "A Widow and her Friends."
  Arriving at Journey's End
  Failing to Find Peace and Quiet in the Country
  A Message from the Outside World
  She Goes into Retirement
  She Goes to the Fancy Dress Ball as Juliet
  She is the Subject of More Hostile Criticism
  She Looks for Relief Among the Old Ones
  Some Think She Remained in Retirement Too Long
  They All Go Skating
  They Take a Morning Run
  And Here Winning New Friends

A Quiet Dinner With Doctor Bottles
Miss Babbles, the Authoress, Calls and
Reads Aloud
Mrs. Diggs is Alarmed at Discovering
Mr. Waddles Arrives Too Late
She is Disturbed by a Vision Which
Appears to be Herself
She Goes Into Colors
She Contemplates the Cloister
She Decides to Die
She Finds That Exercise Does Not
Improve Her Spirit
She Finds Consolation in the Mirror
Fishing
She Becomes a Nurse
Miss Babbles Brings Paper With
Scurrilous Article
Hiawatha, Longfellow poem on back, 10 1/2
inches
Hiawatha, Indian portrait, border is Indians, te-
pees, Hiawatha poem on back, multi-color, 10
1/2 inches
Hiawatha, poem, pitcher, picture of Indian, 7 5/
8 inches
**Islands from Reservoir Hill, East Liverpool,
Ohio,** blue, 10 inches
**Kip-Beekman-Livingston, Hermance House,
Rhinebeck,** (New York), backstamped Souve-
nir 17th Annual Banquet, Duchess County So-
ciety **City of New York, Hotel Astor, January 16, 1913,** tulip border, deep blue, 10 1/2
inches
Martha Washington portrait, imported by Bowman, 1905, blue, 10 inches
Mt. Vernon, imported by Bowman, 1905, blue,
10 inches
**Old Fairbanks House, Dedham, Massachu-
setts,** built in 1662, morning glory border, deep
blue
Pike's Peak, blue, 10 inches
Plattsburg on Lake Champlain, tercentenary
plate, coats of arms of Champlain, multi-color,
10 1/2 inches
Provincial Parliament Building, Victoria, B.C.,
imported by Bowman, blue, 10 inches
White House, the, Washington, D.C., imported
by Bowman, blue, 10 inches

EAST LIVERPOOL
POTTERY COMPANY
East Liverpool, Ohio
1884-1903

This American company made souvenir china for the presidential campaign
of 1896.

ENCO NATIONAL
Importers
New York City
1909

Enco seems to be the only importer
still ordering souvenirs from England. For
many years Enco dealt mostly in trinkets
and souvenir items from Japan. Their
English imports are made by Alfred
Meakin, Ltd. The items resemble the older
Jonroth imports in color and appearance
except for the large printed "blurbs" on
the front of many plates such as "We Made
It" which appears on the Pike's Peak commemorative. The colors are a rich deep
blue or a rather faded pink.

Grand Canyon National Park, Arizona, ashtray, blue, 6 inches
Grant's Farm, St. Louis, Missouri, blue, 9 1/2
inches
Shepherd of the Hills, Branson, Missouri, blue,
9 1/2 inches

FRENCH, MITCHELL,
WOODBURY, COMPANY
Importers
Boston
1901-1905

This short-lived firm imported plates
made by Adams. They all have the same
wide, floral border — although the colors are varied. Most of the scenes are of
places on the East Coast. They are listed
under Adams, although the photos appear
in this section.

WALLIS GIMSON and
COMPANY
Lane Delph Pottery
Fenton Staffordshire, England
1884-1890

This company, in business for only
six years, is somewhat of a mystery. The

firm was Pratt and Simpson, 1878-1873. The mark L.S. and S. was used by Gimson — for what reason is unknown. The examples might have been part of a dinner or tea service rather than a commemorative.

Founders of Our Republic, center is of White House, border shows Washington, Jefferson, Franklin and Lafayette, green, 10 1/4 inches
Governor General's Residence, Ottawa, octagonal, 9 3/4 inches
"The World" dish and lid, lid has Washington portrait and Castle Garden, New York, advertiser described this as ironstone. Godden says this firm made earthenware.

GLASGOW POTTERY COMPANY
Trenton, New Jersey
1863

The Glasgow Pottery, founded in 1863, made quantities of souvenir cups and saucers for Centennial Tea Parties which were held in various sections of the country. Glasgow exhibited at the Centennial in Philadelphia. This company made ironstone, earthenware, and majolica, and also furnished dishes for the United States Marine Corps (stamped USMC), the Navy Quartermaster Dept., and other government agencies.

Battlefield of the Revolution, figures of Liberty and Prosperity, pink with black line around saucer
Boston Tea Party, Philadelphia, 1873, center is printed "Advanced Memento of 1876 Centennial," size? color?
John Hancock, cup and saucer

GREENFIELD POTTERY
location and dates not found

This is obviously a contemporary pottery — not listed in Godden. Plate appears to be of recent manufacture.

Boaron, blue, 9 inches

HALL CHINA COMPANY
East Liverpool Ohio
1903-

The Hall China Company prospered after a rocky beginning and is still in business today. Lois Lehner lists five pages of marks for this company in her book, *U.S. Marks on Pottery, Porcelain and Clay*. The plate listed is backstamped Royal Vitreous Under Glaze with the intertwined initials H. and C.

Pittsburgh Centennial 1809-1909, center is scene of homestead of A. Campbell, (a commemorative of the founding of the Disciples of Christ Church), earthenware, green, 9 inches

HAMPSHIRE POTTERY
Keene, New Hampshire
1876-1916

According to Barber, this pottery made souvenir items for summer resorts. They were usually done in black on a white background.

Landing of the Pilgrims, mug, brown on cream, 4 inches
Landing of the Pilgrims, pitcher, brown and beige, 7 3/4 inches
Map of Long Island and Long Island Sound, rectangular platter

S. HANCOCK and SONS
Stoke on Trent Staffordshire, England
1858-1937

The Hancock mark will be found on early imports by Rowland and Marsellus. Bowman also used this firm.

View of U.S. Capitol, imported by Bowman

GEORGE S. HARKER and COMPANY
East Liverpool, Ohio
1890-1972

Although Harker was in business for nearly one hundred years, most of its souvenir items seem to date from the nineteen twenties. The firm made a vast quantity and variety of dinnerware and other items.

Lincoln and Log Cabin, "Compliments of Zanas Murphy," 6 1/2 inches
Martha Washington, 8 inches
Official Office of President Coolidge, Summer White House, When he Fished the Brule River, 6 inches
Plymouth Rock, blue, 6 inches
Woman's Club Building, Vincennes, Indiana, blue, 6 inches

HOLLAND

This is the only mark on the back of tiles with Boston views. All are six inches square. Beacon Hill, Boston, signed G.M. Goff, '68.

Boston State House
Old Ironsides
Old State House
S.S. Peter Styvesant (ship)

THOMAS HUGHES
Longport, Burslem Staffordshire, England
1860-1957

The one plate found with this mark is identical to plates made by Davenport (same color, size and design).

Lookout Mountain from Chattanooga, blue, 9 5/6 inches

JOHNSON BROTHERS
Hanley, Staffordshire, England
1899-

This pottery is best known in America for a dinner set made just after World War II (1950) called Historic America. Each piece has a center scene showing some event or scene of the early days of the Republic. The border is the acorn and oak leaf which was first used in the 1830s. The colors are blue or pink. Johnson Brothers also made many other commemorative pieces in various colors and styles.

Arizona, Grand Canyon in center, seal of state and ten other scenes in border, pink, blue, black, multi-color, 10 3/4 inches
Boston, views of, acorn border, stamped on back, reg. U.S.pat. office, pat. no. 999155, blue, 10 inches
Capitol, Washington, D.C., 8 3/4 inches
First Fort Dearborn, the, 1833-1933, Century of Progress, made for **Marshall Fields**, purple, 8 3/4 inches, (could be part of a set)
George and Martha Washington, Mt. Vernon and the Capitol, twelve sided, creamy beige
George and Martha Washington, cup and saucer, Mt. Vernon on cup, gold banded, gold handle on cup
Hancock House, Boston, Massachusetts, blue, 6 7/8 inches
Historic America dinner set (salad plates are square)
    Clipper Ship Flying Cloud, 18 inch round chop plate
    New Orleans levee oval dish
    Block House egg cups
    cake plate (see brochure photo)
    mugs large and small
    Ferry Boat bowls
    Natural Bridge of Virginia sauce dish
    San Francisco saucers, regular size and large
    Covered Wagons plates, 6 inches
    Boston Harbor
    Lowell House
    Frozen Up
    Independence Hall
    Michigan Avenue
    Sacramento City, California

Hancock House
Barnum's Museum oval platter
Hudson from West Point
Niagara Falls
President's House, square, 8 inches
San Francisco Harbor cups
Independence Hall, red and gold, made for Tatler and Lanson, Trenton, 8 3/4 inches
Lewis and Clark commemorative, Oregon state seal, scenes of early days, blue or brown, 8 3/4 inches
Montana, blue, 10 inches
Mt. Rushmore, South Dakota, (1960s), blue and other colors
Old Man of the Mountain, blue, 7 inches
Oregon City
Pennsylvania German Folklore Society of Ontario, Canada, pink, 1960
Washington's Headquarters at Newburgh, blue, 8 inches

JONROTH
John H. Roth and Company
Importer
Peoria, Illinois
1909-1970
Florida, 1970-

Jonroth is the trademark of the John Roth Importing Company, which imported souvenirs longer than any other company in the U.S. The firm began operations in 1909 in Peoria, Illinois. Its early imports were the little porcelain novelties shaped like hats, shoes, baskets, etc. These came from Germany. Beginning sometime in the 1920s, the firm began importing plates from England. Perhaps people were becoming tired of the trinkets and were looking for something different. Also the wire plate hanger came on the market about this time. The Ridgway Jonroth items made their first appearance in the 1930s, according to a letter from Royal Doulton which now owns the Ridgway firm. Most Jonroth items were made by Adams but the firm also used Ridgway, Royal Staffordshire, British Anchor, and others. The list of views in this chapter is merely representative. A listing of all the Jonroth views would be a book in itself.

Ash Lawn, Home of President James Monroe, Charlottesville, Virginia, floral border, deep blue, 9 inches
Bar Harbor, Maine, Balanced Rock, Thunder Hole, etc., blue, 9 inches
Bennington, Vermont, similar to five-view styles by Beardmore
Bok Singing Tower, Florida, blue, lavender, 10 inches
Boston Library, blue, pink
Coolidge Home, Plymouth, Vermont, creamer, blue
Cumberland Falls, blue, 10 inches
Estes Park and Rocky Mountain Park, 10 inches
Eternal Light, Peace Monument, Gettysburg, resembles rolled edge Rowland and Marsellus style
Franconia Notch, New Hampshire, blue, 6 and 9 inches
Franconia Notch, the Flume, purple, 7 inches
General Lee's Headquarters
Hermitage, the, 6 3/4 inches
Historic and Picturesque Tennessee, Nashville, capitol building in center, three Tennessee presidents at top, roses border with three scenes, blue, 9 3/4 inches
Home of Mary Washington, 1774-1789, floral border, blue, pink
House of Seven Gables, blue, pink, 7 inches
Lincoln's Birthplace, Hodgenville, Kentucky, blue, 9 inches
Lincoln's Home, Springfield, Illinois, blue, 6, 8, 10 inches
Lincoln's Tomb, Springfield, Illinois, Lincoln Memorial Plate, Farewell Address on back, floral border, blue, 9 3/4 inches
Luray, Virginia, center is Titania's Veil, border is roses and dogwood, 1939, blue, 10 inches
Marblehead, Massachusetts, New York Fleet at Anchor, Old Town House, etc., 6 1/4 inches
Mt. Vernon, floral border, wine red, 10 inches
Narrows, the Wisconsin Dells, Wisconsin, blue, 10 inches
Natural Bridge of Virginia, border has inserts of Washington and Jefferson
Old Cape Cod Windmill, border scenes, pink, 10 inches
Old Church Tower, Jamestown, Virginia, four border scenes, blue, 10 1/2 inches
One Thousand Island International Bridge, multi-color, 10 inches
Pennsylvania Monument, Gettysburg, rolled edge, (dated 12/27) blue, 10 inches
Picturesque 1,000 Islands, pink, blue, 7 1/4 and 9 3/4 inches
Picturesque Keokuk, Iowa, center is lock and dam on Mississippi River, six border scenes with Chief Keokuk portrait at base, (19 impressed date?), blue, 10 inches

Pilgrim Memorial Monument, Providence, Massachusetts, blue, 9 inches

Saratoga Springs, the Spouting Geyser, salt and pepper, blue, 2 1/2 inches tall

St. John's Church, Richmond, Virginia, floral border, deep blue

Snyder Paddle Wheel, blue

Stephen Foster Home, blue

Thousand Islands, floral border, blue, 10 inches

Valley Forge, blue, 9 inches; pink, 10 inches

Williamsburg, Virginia, four border scenes, blue, 10 inches

Williamsburg, Virginia, farmer's cup and saucer, pink

Yorktown, (Historic) Virginia, four border scenes, blue, 9 inches

JONES McDUFFEE and STRATTON
Importers
Boston, Massachusetts
1810-1955

On the back of almost every Wedgwood American-view plate made between 1893 and 1955 will be a little, sometimes indistinct, circle with the words Jones McDuffee, and Stratton, Sole Importers, Boston. This company was in the business of importing ceramics for almost 150 years. The company is now part of a larger firm and no longer imports commemoratives. No Wedgwood collection would be complete without the plate which the company had made in 1910 to commemorate its 100th anniversary

If all the different views were counted, there would be more than 1,500. See the Wedgwood section for more about this firm. Jones, McDuffee and Stratton also imported views made by Adams, Wood, and undoubtedly others.

Plate made for the company's 100th anniversary calendar tile 1928

KETTLESPRING KILNS
Alliance, Ohio
1950-

This American firm makes inexpensive views from designs submitted by regional patriotic and preservation groups. The plates pictured are typical of what is produced. (The company did not respond to a letter requesting background information about the history and activities of the firm.)

KNOWLES, EDWIN M., CHINA COMPANY
Newell, and Chester, West Virginia
1900-1963

This company should not be confused with Knowles, Taylor, and Knowles, which was in business from 1854 to 1931. Both firms ran very successful operations for many years. K.T.K. is remembered for creating the beautiful artware called "Lotus."

Anton Cermak, 1933, blue, 9 1/2 inches (Anton Cermak was the mayor of Chicago who took a bullet meant for President Franklin Roosevelt.)

LAMBERTON-SCAMMELL
Trenton, New Jersey
1893-1954

Few would argue the statement that the most beautiful railroad china ever made was produced by the Scammell China Company (beginning in 1928) to commemorate the 100th anniversary of the Baltimore and Ohio Railroad. The center scenes of this rich blue ware show viaducts, bridges, rivers, etc., associated with the B. and O. The border of the earlier pieces shows a steam powered train, while the later ones show a diesel. This ware is unique among railroad china in that each piece required a separate unit (design). A border and a center scene had to be made for each piece ranging from a tiny saucer to a large platter. All the engravings of the copper plates had to be done by hand, and a whole year was required to prepare the plates. Three months were needed to make each piece which

27

was then fired three times. The company also made china for other railroads, for steamships, church and patriotic groups, etc. Anything marked Shenango is after 1954.

George Washington Inauguration, 1789-1939, backstamped, Official **Souvenir, New York World's Fair, 1939**, blue, 11 inches
Moravian Church, Bethlehem, Pennsylvania, porcelain, pink, 10 1/2 inches
Moravian Historical Plate, "Widow's House, 1767," border includes heads of two men and two women, blue
Queen's County Jockey Club, crest, clubhouse, timer's booth, infield, track, jockeys, etc., platter, 9 1/2 by 12 inches
Trenton, 250th anniversary, 1929, 10 1/2 inches
United States Squadron Before Algiers, blue, 11 inches, after 1955
Washington Bi-centennial, portrait center, scenic border, 11 inches
Willimantic, border shows scenes of Hartford, made for G. Fox and Company, 6 1/2 inches

LAUGHLIN, HOMER, CHINA COMPANY
Newell, West Virginia
1874-

The Laughlin Brothers Pottery was established at East Liverpool, Ohio, in 1874. After 1879 Homer Laughlin became the sole owner of the factory. The firm is still in business today at Newell, West Virginia. The Laughlin Pottery was among the first of the twenty-nine potteries in East Liverpool to make decorated wares. The firm worked with gold trim, tinted background, raised design, etc., and has always specialized in hotel and institutional ware. In 1942 the company made a dinner set called Historical America. According to Mr. E. S. Carson, spokesman for the company, this ware was made exclusively for the F.W. Woolworth Company and was sold throughout the country. These dishes were made in blue and pink, and each one depicts a different scene from American history. The plates

and platters have a floral border with a white gadroon rim.

Historical America
George Washington Takes Command, plate 10 inches
Betsy Ross and Flag, plate 9 inches
Purchase of Manhattan Island, plate 8 inches
Ponce de Leon Discovers Florida, large soup
Liberty bell, plate, 7 inches
Paul Revere plate, 6 inches
Lincoln Rail Splitter, dessert-fruit dish
First Thanksgiving, platter, 13 inches
Steamship Clermont, platter, 11 inches
Pony Express, vegetable dish
Lincoln's Gettysburg Address, oval bowl
Franklin's Experiment, cups
Mayflower, saucers
Stage Coach, cereal bowl
Barbara Fritchie, sugar bowl with lid
Star Spangled Banner, creamer
George Washington and his Family, teapot
Benjamin Godfrey Church, Godfrey, Illinois, black transfer with white della robbia border, 9 1/2 inches
Golden Gate International Exposition, 1939, 10 1/2 inches
New York World's Fair, 1939, 10 inches
White House, 48 state seals in border, 7 inches

LENOX CHINA COMPANY
Trenton, New Jersey
1889-

The best known American china manufacturer, the Lenox China Company, was formed in 1889 as the Ceramic Art Company. From the beginning, the founders were determined to make the best china possible. They struggled for many years to achieve recognition and to show the world that fine china could be made in the United States. Starting about 1900, the company made commemorative items such as plates, pitchers, tobies, tea sets, etc. These were always made in limited quantities for specific occasions. The company is still manufacturing fine china and commemoratives.

Alamo, the, San Antonio, Texas, gold edge, brown on cream, 1937, 10 1/2 inches

Architect's tea set, commissioned in 1933 by a group in Washington, D.C., for the benefit of those in the creative arts, 12 cups and saucers, 11 lunch plates, sugar, creamer, waste bowl, tea pot; all are decorated in copper lustre, the lids have copper lustre dove finials, serving pieces bear the Great Seal of the United States, all except the waste bowl have scenes of important American historical buildings

Boston State House, 1849, gold edge, brown on cream, 1933, 10 1/2 inches

Chicago, South Water Street, 1832, gold edge, brown on cream, 10 1/2 inches

Civil War plates,(set of 10), 2500 sets made, (Confederacy scenes)
    The Great Seal of the Confederacy
    The White House of the Confederacy
    Lee and Jackson
    A Call to Arms
    The Merrimac
    The "General" (a steam locomotive)
    J.E.B. Stuart
    Confederate Camp
    Blockade Runner
    Fort Sumter

Columbia University, Law Library, 1932, (part of a set?)

Historical Homes, made for Colonial Dames, set of 12, sepia, 10 1/2 inches

Museum of the Confederacy in Richmond, Virginia, set of 12 in color (1201 sets made), bone china, all different

Nevada, covered wagon scene, creamer, back has gold stars and eagle, decorated by P.C. Patchin, sepia and gold, 5 1/2 inches from spout to back of handle

Old Fort Dearborn, Chicago in 1857, mug, decorated by Patchin, mulberry, sepia, and gold, 3 1/4 inches

Old Spanish Courthouse, New Orleans, mug, decorated by Patchin, sepia and gold, 3 1/2 inches

Old State House, Delaware, signed Barbara McBride, one of a series, pen and ink drawings, eagles and plows at bottom, silver rim

Post Office, New York, 1830, coffee pot, decorated by Patchin, sepia and gold, 8 inches high

San Luis Rey Francia, c. 1802, gold edge, brown on cream, 1933, 10 1/2 inches

Santa Barbara Mission, California, mug, decorated by Patchin, sepia and gold, 3 1/4 inches

Saratoga Springs, New York, 1839, mug, decorated by Patchin, sepia and gold, 3 1/2 inches

State House, Montpelier, Vermont, mugs, decorated by Patchin, 1933, 3 1/4 inches

Tamany Hall, New York, mug, Patchin decorated, sepia and gold, 3 1/4 inches

Tomb of Washington, two handled bowl, black, gold eagle and stars, 4 inches diameter, 3 3/4 inches high

Washington Silhouette, gold and black, stars around medallion and border, 1732-1932, set of six, 10 1/2 inches

William Penn, toby, natural coloring, three quarter figural, 6 1/4 inches tall

Yale, bowl, 1914, replica of football stadium

LIMOGES CHINA COMPANY
Sebring, Ohio
1900-1955

The Limoges China Company is best know for the quantity and quality of the dinnerware produced during their fifty years in business. The firm made a few commemoratives, probably all before World War II.

Lindbergh

Eiffel Tower

Statue of Liberty, square

Scenes from Revolution, signed and dated, 1894, all different, one is Lydia Darrah Discovers British Plan of Attack, Warns Minute Men

Young's Million Dollar Pier, from the south, Atlantic City, New Jersey, blue, 10 inches

L.S. and S.
Germany

The mark L.S. and S. appears on the back of a small earthenware plate with a scene of the U. S. Government Building at the World's Columbian Exposition in 1893.

MAASTRICHT
see Petrus Regout

JOHN MADDOCK and SONS
Burslem Staffordshire, England
1855

Although this company has been in business for more than one hundred and forty years, little was made in the way of souvenir ware. The only piece found is a square, cut-cornered blue plate, marked, "Commemorating the Visit of Their Majesties to the U.S. in 1939."

THOMAS MADDOCK AND SONS
Trenton, New Jersey
1869-1893

This American firm made mostly ironstone. Maddock owned and operated another works in Trenton, the Maddock Pottery Company, which made semi-porcelain. The second named company probably made the items listed. In 1893 the company became Lamberton-Scammell.

George Washington pitcher, portrait with silver lustre rim, marked Patriotic Order, Sons of America, Sept. 1913, twenty-fifth annual meeting, State Camp of New Jersey, 11 1/2 inches
Lackawanna R.A.C. no. 185, 50th Annual, 1856-1904, maroon and gold stripes, 9 5/8 inches
Masonic plate, Zembo Temple, Harrisburg, Pa., 9 1/2 inches

MASON'S
Hanley Staffordshire, England
1862-

The word Mason's has been used by the G.L. Ashworth and Brothers Pottery since it took over the old Morley works in 1872. Morley and Ashworth are best remembered for their famous American Marine Pattern. The name Mason has been used with and without the Ashworth name since 1932. The company is now part of the Wedgwood group.

Capitol in center, George Washington and eagle in border, signed H. Fennell, pink, 10 1/2 inches; same, blue, with gadroon rim.
Dominion of Canada, multi-colored, 10 inches

Niagara Falls, souvenir of, Canada, brown, 10 1/2 inches
U.S. Capitol, views of, purple, gadroon rim. 10 1/2 inches
University of Western Ontario Jubilee 1938
World's Fair, 1939 (ironstone)

D.E. McNICOL POTTERY
East Liverpool, Ohio
1892-1960s

This was another Ohio pottery which seemed to be most active in the late nineteenth century. The company made small plates in various colors and also children's dishes.

Clarksburg, West Virginia, 7 inches
Lutheran Orphan's Home, Topton, Pa., green with gold border, 7 inches
Peace, WWI, Allied flags, 7 1/2 inches
Washington, Jefferson, Lafayette, Napoleon, crossed American flags and shield in center

ALFRED MEAKIN, LTD.
Tunstall Staffordshire, England
1875-

Anyone who has ever collected ironstone in even the most casual way is familiar with the Meakin name. There were and are several Meakin companies which carried on a large trade with the United States for many years. The Alfred Meakin Company is now one of the major suppliers of commemoratives from England. The company makes plates and other items for ENCO. It would be impossible even to begin to list all the views. The items are generally well-made and attractive.

Beauvoir House, Jefferson Davis Shrine contemporary plate
Cypress Gardens, blue, 4 1/2 inches

J. and G. MEAKIN
Hanley Staffordshire, England
1851-

This Meakin pottery seems to have made only one commemorative as far as may be determined.

World's Fair, 1939, blue, 10 1/4 inches

MELLOR and COMPANY
Trenton, New Jersey
1884-1959

Mellor and Company was a mark used by the Cook Pottery Company to avoid confusion between its factory and the old Crescent Pottery, and also to honor one of its founders, F.G. Mellor.

Rhode Island State Capitol, embossed, medium blue, 8 1/2 inches

MERCER POTTERY COMPANY
Trenton, New Jersey
1868-1938

Mercer claimed to be the first pottery in this country to make semi-porcelain. The firm used at least 12 different marks at various times.

Historic Trenton, souvenir of, 250th anniversary of Trenton, blue, 9 inches
Washington's Headquarters, Newburgh, New York, 1783-1883, blue, 7 1/2 inches

MINTON
Stoke Staffordshire
1793-

This famous old firm supposedly made commemorative tiles and plates for the Centennial Exposition of 1876, but none were found in the sources checked.

The company did make numerous tiles and plates for the American market for many years. The items are generally dated with an incised mark. These marks are in Godden's book of pottery and porcelain marks. The letter "S" was added in 1873 (Minton's). The firm is now part of Royal Doulton, Ltd.

Arnold's Mansion, blue, 9 3/4 inches
Bertram's House, blue, 9 inches, imported by Wright, Tyndal, and Van Roden, before 1910
Betsy Ross House, blue, 9 inches, imported by Wright, Tyndal, and Van Roden before 1910
Billerica, Massachusetts, a series dated 1905, floral border, blue, 10 inches
    Aqueduct
    Middlesex
    Canal over Shasheen River
    250th Anniversary
    Old Oak Tree
    First Parish Meeting House
Burlingham, Massachusetts, Meeting House, blue, 9 3/4 inches
Birthplace of Oliver Wendell Holmes, Cambridge, Mass., tile, black or brown, square, 6 inches
Boston State House as seen in 1818, tile, framed, blue
Carpenter's Hall, floral and trellis border, blue, 9 3/4 inches
Christ Church, blue, 9 inches
Cliff House and Seal Rocks (San Francisco?)
First Church, Quincy, Massachusetts
Framingham Normal, Massachusetts, pink
Girard College, Philadelphia, c. 1910, deep blue, 10 inches
Golden Gate Park, Strawberry Hill
House of the Seven Gables, blue, 10 inches
Interstate Industrial Exposition, Chicago, tile, 1880
Landing of General Lafayette, Castle Garden, 1824, blue, 9 1/2 inches
New Bedford, tile, as seen in 1767
Old Hancock House, Beacon Street, Boston, blue, 6 inches; tile, sepia, 6 inches; tile, red, marked 1773-1873, 6 inches
Old Meeting House, Hingham, Mass., 1887
Old Nantucket, tile, blue
Old Tower, Newport Tower, tile, grey-blue
Penn's Treaty, blue, 9 3/4 inches
Penn's Treaty Tree, blue, 9 1/2 inches
Philadelphia, scenes of, set of four, blue with gold rim 9 1/2 inches
    State House
    Water Works
    others?

Queen Isabella Pledging her Jewels, Columbus, etc., tile, 6 inches

Salem, Mass., House of the Seven Gables, elaborate scrolled and floral border, backstamped, to commemorate the 200th anniversary of the incorporation of the town, May 10, 1905, deep blue, 10 1/2 inches

Santa Barbara Mission, California, A.D. 1776, floral border, blue, 10 1/2 inches

S.S. Mauretania in New York Harbor with tugboat Sandy Hook, floral border, insignia of Cunard Steamship Company, blue, 9 inches

Stenton, 1901, blue, 9 1/2 inches

Sunbury House on the Nashaminy, blue, 9 1/2 inches

Washington's Headquarters at Valley Forge, blue, 9 3/4 inches

Wharten House, the scene of 1776, blue, 9 3/4 inches

William Penn Cottage, Laticia Court, blue, 9 1/2 inches (part of Philadelphia set?)

NORCROSS, MELLEN and COMPANY
Sole Importers
Boston
1897

This seems to have been another short lived importing company which, seeing the success of Jones, McDuffee and Stratten and Rowland and Marsellus, decided this would be a profitable business. The company could have been affiliated with some of the large department store chains of the time.

OLD HISTORICAL BLUE PLATE COMPANY
England

This company name could not be found in marks books. It probably was a trade name used by one of the larger importers. (Some are marked Rowland and Marsellus-see Rowland and Marsellus section.)

Milwaukee City Hall
Pilgrim Monument, Provincetown, Mass.
Plymouth, Mass., coupe shape
William Pepperell House, 1733

PETRUS REGOUT and COMPANY
Maastricht, Holland
1834-1968

Petrus Regout founded a ceramics works at Maastricht, Holland, in 1834. In 1879 the firm became Petrus Regout and Company and began using a sphinx as part of its trademark. Another ceramics works in Maastricht, formed in 1859, was the Societe Ceramique. Regout did not make a great many commemoratives for the American market, and what was made was in direct imitation of the English product.

Allied Liberation of Holland, Maastricht was first city liberated by the Allies, marked Sept. 14, 1944, American soldier in center, flags, etc. in border, blue, 8 inches

British, Dutch, American flags in center, stone bridge and roof tops in border, colorful, Sept. 9, 1944, 9 inches (same occasion as first entry)

Illinois State Capitol, Springfield, made in medium and deep blue (border is big roses), 9 3/4 inches

Indiana Soldiers and Sailors Monument, Indianapolis, deep blue, (border is eight floral panels), 9 3/4 inches

Lincoln's House, Springfield, Illinois, Lincoln in oval inset at upper right, floral border, made in 1909 to commemorate the 100th anniversary of Lincoln's birth, blue, 9 1/2 inches, (there are three versions of this plate, the borders are different, but the center is the same. Also one version has a green border with a blue center.)

Mt. Vernon and Washington, blue, 9 1/2 inches, one version has eight paneled floral border, other has large roses

State House, Indianapolis, Indiana, paneled floral border, blue, 9 1/2 inches

POPE GOSSER
Coshocton, Ohio
1902-1958

This firm was known for its innovative fine quality china. The plate pictured is a prime example—a beautiful view of Lafayette, Indiana, made for its 100th anniversary. The center shows the founder of the town. Border scenes show various monuments and buildings. At the bottom of the plate is the first verse of "The Banks of the Wabash" by Paul Dresser. The plate is porcelain, clear, bright blue, 10 inches.

R.G.

This was the only mark on the back of a seven inch plate of San Francisco, dated 1910.

R.M.D.

Another mystery mark—the only item found was a Landing of Hendrick Hudson, blue, 10 inch plate.

RIDGWAY'S
Bedford Works, Hanley
Staffordshire, England
1879-1920 RIDGWAY'S, LTD.
1920-1962 RIDGWAY POTTERIES, LTD.
1955-

The Ridgway Potteries have been making commemoratives since the early years of the twentieth century. The company was represented for many years by the Rowland and Marsellus Importing Company and later by Jonroth. During the teens and perhaps earlier, the firm made a distinctive commemorative in shades of brown with lustre edging. There are tiles, mugs, etc. The company is now a part of the Royal Doulton Group.

Beehive Store, (name of town not given) pre-1900 mark: Ridgway bow and quiver, three-story building in center, background is little stars and stripes, blue, 10 inches

Boothbay Harbor, brown with gold rim, 9 inches

Capitol, Washington, D.C., tile, black and yellow-brown glaze, silver lustre rim, square, 6 1/2 inches; plate, brown

Capitol and Mt. Vernon, views of, mug, black on yellow-brown, silver handle and trim, 4 inches tall

City Hall, New York City, blue

Landing of the Pilgrims, border scenes, rolled edge, (imported by Bosselman) blue, 10 inches

Martha Washington portrait, blue, 10 inches

Mormon Temple Square, rich brown, 5 1/2 inches

Mt. Vernon, brown lustre, 10 inches

Minnesota, State Capitol, 6 border scenes, blue

Nation's Capitol, brown lustre, 10 inches

New Capitol, Albany, New York, floral border, 1933, imported by Van Heusen Charles Company, blue, 9 1/2 inches

Omaha Auditorium, blue, 9 inches

Plymouth, Massachusetts, rolled edge, blue, (imported by Bossleman) blue, 10 inches

State House, where?, blue, 9 inches

Statue of Liberty

U.S. Capitol seven plates
   Capitol
   Mt. Vernon
   Arlington
   Library of Congress
   Treasury
   White House
   Washington Monument

U.S. Capitol, shades of brown, rim has berries and vine motif, (marked Ridgway Royal Semiporcelain) 1905-1912

Washington's Headquarters, green and amber

ROWLAND and MARSELLUS
Importers
New York
1893-1937

This firm, in business for forty years, was Jones, McDuffee and Stratton's closest competitor. Rowland and Marsellus imported an almost unbelievable number of plates, vases, tumblers, cups and saucers, and other items, mostly in deep blue, but sometimes in other colors. The company's method of backstamping has caused no end of confusion. Laidacker and other respected authorities stated that Rowland and Marsellus was an English pottery. The mistake is understandable when one studies the backstamp. The initials R and M are arranged in a diamond. Seldom if ever is the name of the manufacturer given. Until about 1910 Hancock was the maker, but after that the company used Royal Fenton and others. The two features most commonly associated with Rowland and Marsellus are the fruit and flower border and the rolled edge.

The fruit and flower border was taken directly from an old pre-1830 blue Staffordshire pattern. The origin of the rolled edge is somewhat of a mystery as there does not seem to be any practical reason for such a design. There would be more room for the secondary scenes.

David Ringering of Salem, Oregon has compiled the most complete and comprehensive list of Rowland and Marsellus. He has also compiled much background information about the firm and its history.

The lists are divided into five categories-fruit and flower border, coupe shape plates, odd items including cups and saucers, rolled edge plates, and Ye Old Historical Pottery plates.

Fruit and Flower Border Plates—all are 10 inches—all are blue—additional colors noted

Altoona, Pennsylvania, Horseshoe Curve
Battle of Bunker Hill (brown)
Battle of Concord Bridge
Battle of Germantown
Battle of Lake Erie
Biltmore House, Asheville, North Carolina
Block House, four sides
Block House, six sides
Boston Harbor
Boston Massacre, March, 5, 1770 and Old State House (green)
Bunker Hill Monument, Charlestown, Massachusetts
Capitol, Washington, D.C.
City Hall, Lowell, Massachusetts
Clara Barton Birthplace, North Oxford, Massachusetts
Commodore John Paul Jones Capturing the Serapis, September 23rd, 1779
DeSoto's Discovery of the Mississippi, 1541
Don't Give Up the Ship, Death of Captain Lawrence, June 1st, 1813
Ellsworth Homestead, Daughters of the American Revolution, 1907
Elm at Cambridge Massachusetts, Where Washington Took Command of the American Army, July 3rd, 1775 (pink)
Faneuil Hall, Boston

Faneuil Hall, Boston, From the Harbor
Federal Hall, Wall Street, Where Washington Took Oath of Office as First President, April, 30th, 1789
Hermitage, Home of Andrew Jackson
Home of George Washington, Mount Vernon
Horseshoe Curve (same as Altoona?) (green)
Independence Hall, Philadelphia, Pennsylvania, Where the Declaration of Independence was Signed, July 4, 1776 (green)
John Alden and Priscilla (brown) (multi-color)
Landing of the Pilgrims
Landing of Roger Williams, 1636
Massachusetts State House, Boston, Massachusetts
Mayflower in Plymouth Harbor
Memorial and Public Library, Westerly, Rhode Island
Minneapolis, Minnesota, state capitol
Molly Pitcher At Battle of Monmouth, June 28, 1776
National Monument to the Forefathers
New Library at Boston
Niagara Falls
Old City Gates, St. Augustine
Old Stone Mill, Newport, Rhode Island
Old South Church, Boston, Massachusetts
Oliver and Abigail (Wolcott) Ellsworth, D.A.R., Windsor, Connecticut, 1906 (same as Ellsworth Homestead?)
Patrick Henry Addressing the Virginia Assembly and St. John's Church, Richmond, Virginia
Plymouth Rock
Plymouth Rock, same as above except for addition of stars around center scene
Retreat of the British from Concord, April 19, 1775
Ride of Paul Revere, April 18, 1775
Shaw Mansion, New London, Connecticut, 1907
Souvenir of Delaware Water Gap from Winona Cliff
Standish House, Duxbury, Massachusetts, 1666
Surrender of Col. Wm. Ledyard, D.A.R. (The Massacre of Fort Griswold, Groton, Connecticut, Sept. 6, 1781)
Waltham Watch Factory, Waltham, Massachusetts
Washington Crossing the Delaware, Dec. 25, 1776
Washington's Prayer at Valley Forge, 1777 (grey) (green)
Watch Hill Light, Rock and Point
Whirlpool Rapids
White House, Washington, D.C.
Why Don't You Speak for Yourself, John? Priscilla and John Alden
William Penn's Treaty with the Indians

Rolled Edge Plates, most are ten inches, all are blue, additional colors noted. There are nearly 200 known views with the rolled edge border. Not all are Rowland and Marsellus. Check Bosselman, British Anchor, and Bawo and Dotter lists. The phrase "souvenir of" or "view of" has been eliminated.

Alaska-Yukon-Pacific Exposition, Seattle, 1909
Albany, New York State Capitol
Albany, New York, Fort Frederick, State Street in 1775
Allentown, Pennsylvania, the Pike
Altoona, Pennsylvania, Horseshoe Curve
Arlington, Virginia
Asbury Park, New Jersey, the Casino (multicolor)
Atlantic City, New Jersey, Bathing Hour (multicolor)
Baltimore, Maryland, Court House
Baltimore, Indiana, Court House, (misprint)
Bangor, Maine, River Front
Battle Creek, Michigan, B.C. Sanitarium
Bermuda, Alias Somers Islands, Islands of the Great Sound
Bermuda, Alias Somers Island, 1609-1909
Bermuda, Royal Palms, Hamilton, Bermuda
Boston, Massachusetts, Tremont Street Mall
Boston, Massachusetts (Historical) Faneuil Hall
Bridgeport, Connecticut, Soldiers Monument at Seaside Park
Brooklyn, New York, New York and Brooklyn Bridge
Buffalo, New York, Buffalo Library and Soldiers Monument, Lafayette Square
Burns, Robert, portrait
Butte, Montana, Bronco Busting
Canada, La Patrie
Carlisle, Pennsylvania, New Denny Hall
Charlestown, West Virginia, State Capitol
Charlotte, North Carolina, Independence Monument and County Court House
Chicago, Illinois, State Street (green)
Chicago, Illinois, Old Fort Dearborn, Site of Chicago in 1894
Cincinnati, Ohio, City Hall
Cleveland, Ohio, Garfield Memorial
Columbus, Ohio, Ohio State Capitol
Cornell College, Sage Walk
Coven Hoven, Canada, Sir Van Horne's Residence
Dallas, Texas, Confederate Monument
Decatur, Illinois, Illinois Cornfield
Denver, Colorado, Capitol Building
Detroit, Michigan, City Hall
Detroit, Michigan, Log Cabin at Palmer Park
Diaz, Porfirio, portrait-Mexican general
Dickens, Charles, portrait

Fall, River, Massachusetts, Public High School
Fort Williams, Ontario, Canada, Kakabeka Gorge
Gettysburg, Pennsylvania, Pennsylvania State Monument
Golden Rule Company, Golden Rule Company Store (multi-color)
Gloucester, Massachusetts
Grand Rapids, Michigan, City Hall
Hamburg, Germany, Hamburg Rathbus
Hamilton, Canada, Gore Park
Harrisburg, Pennsylvania, New Capitol Building
Hartford, Connecticut, The State Capitol, 1903
Haverhill, Massachusetts, Merrimack Street
Hot Springs, Virginia, The Homestead
Hudson River, Landing of Hendrick Hudson
Indianapolis, Indiana, Soldiers and Sailors Monument
Jackson, Mississippi, New Capitol
Kalamazoo, Michigan, Court House
Kansas City, Missouri, Convention Hall
Lake Champlain, New York, Au Sable Chasm
Lake George, New York, Paradise Bay
Lakewood, New Jersey, Cathedral Drive
Landing of Hendrick Hudson
Leavenworth, Kansas, Evening by Lake Jeannette, Soldiers Home
Lenox, Massachusetts, Nathaniel Hawthorne Cottage, The Little Red House
Lewis and Clark Centennial, 1905
Lima, Ohio, Memorial Hall (multi-color)
Lincoln, Abraham, portrait Lincoln, Nebraska, State Capitol
London, England, St. Paul's Cathedral
Longfellow's Early Home, Portland, Maine
Lookout Mountain, Tennessee, Point Park Entrance
Louisville, Kentucky?
Los Angeles, California, Court House
Memphis, Tennessee, Skyscraper District
Milwaukee, Wisconsin, City Hall
Minneapolis, Minnesota, Minnehaha Falls
Minneapolis, Minnesota, Post Office
Mobile, Alabama, Courthouse and Government Street
Montreal, Canada, Dominion Square (pink)
Nantucket, Massachusetts, Built 1746 (two views-have slightly different borders)
Nashville, Tennessee, Capitol
Newark, New Jersey, City Hall (two views-different borders)
Newport, Rhode Island, Old Stone Mill
New Bedford, Massachusetts, Whaling Monument
New Bedford, Wharf Scene in Old Whaling Days
New London, Connecticut, The Market Place
New Orleans, Louisiana, Canal Street (multicolor)

New York, New York, Statue of Liberty

Niagara Falls, New York, General View of the Falls

Norristown, Pennsylvania, 100th Anniversary 1812-1912

Omaha, Nebraska, The Omaha Auditorium

Onset, Massachusetts, "Meet me on Cape Cod" (two fishermen)

Panama-Pacific International Exposition, San Francisco, 1915, Horticulture Building

Peoria, Illinois, Peoria County Courthouse

Philadelphia, Pennsylvania, City Hall

Philadelphia, Pennsylvania, (Historical) Independence Hall, 1776 (green)

Phoenix, Arizona, ?

Pittsburgh, Pennsylvania, Allegheny County Court House

Plymouth, Massachusetts, Return of the Mayflower (green)

Plymouth Rock 1620

Portland, Maine, City Hall

Portland, Maine, Longfellow's House 1785

Portland, Oregon, Mount Hood from Wooded Hillside

Portland, Oregon, Mount Hood with Lost Lake

Prince Powhatani (portrait of Pocahontas as Rebecca Rolfe)

Providence, Rhode Island, State House

Provincetown, Massachusetts, Pilgrim Memorial Monument (green) (multi-color)

Put-in-Bay, Ohio, Comm. Perry Transferring His Flag, Sept. 10, 1813

Quincy, Illinois, Adams County Courthouse

Richfield Springs, New York, The Park

Richmond, Virginia City Hall

Richmond, Virginia, New State Capitol

Rochester, New York, ?

Roosevelt, Theodore portrait of 26th president

Sag Harbor, Long Island, New York, High School

Salem, Massachusetts, Witch House Built in 1634 (two views,different borders)

Salt Lake, (Utah) Temple Square, Salt Lake City

San Francisco, California, Golden Gate and Entrance to San Francisco Bay (brown)

Saratoga, New York, Saratoga Lake

Scranton, Pennsylvania, Court House (multi-colored)

Seattle, Washington, Carnegie Library

Shakespeare, William, portrait

Sherbrooke, Quebec, Head Office Eastern Townships Bank

Smith, Captayne, John, portrait

Spokane, Washington, Lower Falls

Standish, Myles, Monument, (green)

St. Augustine, Old City Gates

St. Joseph, Missouri, Grand Council of Missouri, June 5 and 6, 1907

St. Louis, Missouri, City Hall

St. Louis, Missouri, City Hall dated 1909 (Centennial plate)

St. Patrick's Cathedral, Harrisburg, Pennsylvania, dedicated 1906

St. Paul, Minnesota, Minnesota State Capitol

St. Paul's Union Church, Trexlertown, Pennsylvania, built 1922

St. Peter's Reformed Church, New, Rittersville, Pennsylvania, 1914

Syracuse, New York, Indian Portrait

Syracuse, New York, Horse Racing at the State Fairgrounds

Tacoma, Washington, Mount Tacoma, 15,000 ft.

Taft, William Howard, and Sherman, James S. portraits

Tampa, Florida, Tampa Bay Hotel

Thousand Islands, New York

1000 Islands House, Alexander Bay, New York

Toledo, Ohio, McKinley Monument

Topeka, Kansas, Capitol

Toronto, Canada, City Hall (multi-color)

Troy, New York, Emma Willard School

Trenton, New Jersey, ?

Valley Forge, Pennsylvania, Washington's Headquarters, summer scene, Dec. 19, 1910

Valley Forge, Pennsylvania, Washington's Headquarters, winter scene, Dec. 19, 1910

Vassar College, General View

Washington, D.C., The Capitol, East Front

Waterbury, Connecticut, The Green

West Point, New Soldier's Monument

White Mountains, New Hampshire, The Old Man of the Mountain, Franconia Notch

Wilkes-Barre, Pennsylvania, The New Court House

Williams College, The Gymnasium

Williamsport, Pennsylvania, City Hall

Winnegar's Store, Grand Rapids, Michigan

Winnipeg, Manitoba, The Canadian Buffalo

Worcester, Massachusetts, City Hall

World's Fair, St. Louis, Missouri, 1904

Yale, New Haven, Connecticut, Old Brick Row

Yarmouth, Nova Scotia, sailing ship

Zanesville, Ohio, Y Bridge

Zion's Union Church, Perry Township, Berks County, Pennsylvania

Coupe shape plates were made in two sizes— six and ten inches. Some collectors pass them by because they do not appear to be as old as they really are. Some go back to the beginning of the twentieth century and were a staple of the Burbank and Low Companies of Plymouth, Massachusetts.

6-inch Coupe Shape Plates

Burlington, Vermont, DeChamplain (brown)

Chicago

Cooperstown, New York, Leather Stocking (James Fenimore Cooper tales)
Denver, five scenes with Elk Seal
Early Missions of California, Five California Missions (green)
Fresno, California, Public Library and 4 other scenes
Jamestown, Virginia, Exposition, 1907, Administration Building (brown) (green)
Jamestown and Norfolk, Virginia, state seal
Mayflower in Plymouth Harbor, Pilgrim Family Names
Montreal, Royal Victoria Cottage (green)
New Bedford, Massachusetts, five scenes
Niagara Falls, Beauty Spots of, view from Steel Arch Bridge
Plymouth Rock, Massachusetts, Canopy Over Plymouth Rock, Pilgrim Family Names, Plymouth Rock, Massachusetts, Canopy Over Plymouth Rock, same as above without names (green)
Plymouth, Massachusetts, five scenes 1906
Richfield Springs, Band Stand in Park
Salem, Massachusetts, Witch and five scenes
Salt Lake City, Mormon Temple (flat plate, 5 3/4 inches)
San Antonio, Texas, The Alamo
Toronto, five scenes
Tuscon, Arizona, five scenes
Vancouver, British Columbia, Beauty Spots of, five scenes
Washington, D.C., Capitol
Yale, University Seal

10 inch coupe shape plates

Alaska-Yukon-Pacific Exposition, Seattle, 1909, four different plates for various stores in Seattle
American Composers
American Poets, 7 portraits (black)
Annapolis Basin, Nova Scotia, Panoramic View
Asheville, North Carolina, Biltmore House (pink)
California, Beauty Spots of, Avalon-Catalina Island (pink)
Denver
Famous Musicians and Composers, 9 portraits
Grand Rapids, Michigan
Harrisburg, Pennsylvania, New Capitol Building
Jamestown and Norfolk, Virginia, Administration Building
Lakewood, New Jersey, Cathedral Drive
Long Island, New York, Wave Crest
Minneapolis, Minnesota, Minnehaha Falls, ribbon border
Minneapolis, Minnesota, Minnehaha Falls, wheat border
Miami, Florida, Chief Osceola

Palm Beach, Florida, Royal Ponciana Hotel
Plymouth, Massachusetts, Return of the Mayflower
Portland, Oregon, Mount Hood
San Antonio, Texas, 6 scenes
San Francisco, California, Harbor Scene
Yale, Old Brick Row

9" plates

This list of plates has only two constants. All are blue and all are 9 inches in size. There are various borders and shades of blue ranging from dull slate to a deep royal blue. Some are part of the Ye Olde Historical Pottery Series (or printed as The Old Historical Pottery series), some are marked British Anchor and some have no marks at all except for "England." The manufacturer or importer (if known) is listed last.

Albany, State Capitol R and M
Albany, State Capitol
Albany, State Capitol different border
Allentown, Pennsylvania, The Square
Altoona, Pennsylvania, Horseshoe Curve
Asbury Park, New Jersey, Casino
Atlantic City, New Jersey, Bathing Hour
Auburn, New York, Post Office, Woods and Sons
Baltimore, Maryland, Washington Monument, R and M
Battle of New Orleans, No. 10. Ye Old Historical Pottery
Bangor, Maine, Court House
Bath, Maine, City of Ships, R and M
Bethlehem, Pennsylvania, Moravian College
Biddeford, Maine, City Building, British Anchor, 1913
Birmingham, Alabama, Tutwiler Hotel
Boston, Massachusetts, State House
Boston, Massachusetts, State House Erected July 4th, 1788, R and M, Ye Olde Blue Plate Co.
Bridgeport, Connecticut, The Stratford Hotel
Bridgeport, Connecticut, Soldiers Monument at Seaside Park
Bunker Hill Monument, Charleston, Massachusetts, No. 1. Ye Olde Historical Pottery
Burlington, Vermont, Post Office
Canton, Ohio, The McKinley National Memorial, R and M
Cape Cod, Oldest Windmill on Cape Cod
Cape Cod, Fishermen
Chatham Cape Cod, The Twin Lights
Chicago, Illinois, New North-Western Railroad Depot
Cincinnati, Ohio, Fountain Square, R and M
Cleveland, Ohio, The New City Hall
Cleveland, Ohio, Garfield Memorial

Columbus, Ohio, State Capitol
Dallas, Texas, Confederate Monument
Delaware Water Gap, Pennsylvania, R and M
Denver, Colorado, State Capitol
Des Moines, Iowa, State Capitol, R and M
De Soto's Discovery of the Mississippi, 1541, No. 11. Ye Old Historical Pottery
Detroit, Michigan, Entrance to Detroit River Tunnel
Detroit. Michigan, City Hall
East Liberty, Pennsylvania, Entrance to Highland Park
Erie, Pennsylvania, Court House
Fall River, Massachusetts, City Hall
Faneuil Hall, Boston, Massachusetts, No. 1. Ye Olde Historical Pottery
Flint, Michigan, City Hall
Fort Dearborn, Site of Chicago in 1804, No. 12. Ye Olde Historical Pottery
Galesburg, Illinois, Court House
Glen Falls New York, (Monument) Battle of Lake George
Gloucester, Massachusetts, Eastern Point Light, British Anchor, 1916
Hamilton, Canada, Court House, British Anchor, 1913
Harrisburg, Pennsylvania, State Capitol
Hartford, Connecticut, The State Capitol
Haverhill, Massachusetts, Whittier's Birthplace, R and M
Independence Hall, 1776, No. 2. Ye Old Historical Pottery
Ithaca, New York, Sage College
Jamestown, New York, Prendergast Free Library
Kingston, Ontario, City Buildings
La Crosse, Wisconsin, Post Office
Lake Placid, Adirondacks, New York, White Face Mountain and Birch Point, The Olde Historical Blue Plate Co.
Lakewood, New Jersey, Lovers Lane, R and M
Landing of Hendrick Hudson, No. 5. Ye Old Historical Pottery
Landing of the Pilgrims, No. 6. Ye Old Historical Pottery
Landing of Roger Williams, No. 3. Ye Old Historical Pottery
Longfellow, Henry W., R and M, The Olde Historical Blue Plate Co.
Los Angeles, California, Court House
Louisville, Kentucky, Boone Monument
Lowell, Massachusetts, Court House
Lynn, Massachusetts, City Hall
Marblehead, Massachusetts, Old Town House, Built 1777, Ye Olde Historical Pottery
Milwaukee, Wisconsin, Post Office and Government Building
Minneapolis, Minnesota, Minnehaha Falls
Mohawk Indian, Mohawk Trail Through the Berkshires, R and M

Montreal, P.Q., City Hall and Market Place
Nantucket County, Massachusetts, Map of County, R and M
Newark, New Jersey, City Hall
Newburgh, New York, Washington's Headquarters
Newport, Rhode Island, Old Stone Mill
New Bedford, Massachusetts, County Court House
New Haven, Connecticut, Court House
New London, Connecticut, State Street from the Railroad Station
New Orleans, Louisiana, Old City Hall
New York, New York, City Hall
New York City, Woolworth Building, The Tallest Building in the World
Niagara Falls, Maid of the Mist (touring boat)
Niagara Falls, New York, General View, No. 16. Ye Olde Historical Pottery
Norristown, Pennsylvania, 100th Anniversary, 1812-1912, R and M
Old North Church, Boston, Massachusetts, No. 1B. Ye Olde Historical Pottery
Orlean, New York, Twin Sisters Rock, Rock City, New York
Omaha, Nebraska, Omaha Auditorium
Patrick Henry Addressing Virginia Assembly 1765, No. 9. Ye Olde Historical Pottery
Perry's Victory on Lake Erie, No. 4. Ye Old Historical Pottery
Philadelphia, Pennsylvania, University of Pennsylvania
Philadelphia, Pennsylvania, Independence Hall, Barry Statue
Pittsburgh, Pennsylvania, Old Block House
Pittsfield, Massachusetts, U.S. Post Office
Plattsburg, New York, Battle of Lake Champlain
Plymouth, Massachusetts, Forefathers Monument
Portland, Maine, City Hall
Portland, Maine, Longfellow's Home
Poughkeepsie, New York, Main Entrance to Vassar College
Poughkeepsie, New York, Steamer Robert Fulton
Providence, Rhode Island, State House
Provincetown, Massachusetts, Pilgrim Monument
Provincetown, Massachusetts, Pilgrim Memorial Monument Dedicated August 5, 1910, (green), The Old Historical Blue Plate Co.
Put-in-Bay, Ohio, Perry Memorial, 1813-1913, Put-in-Bay
Reading, Pennsylvania, Drinking Fountain, City Park
Rip Van Winkle, The Awakening
Rochester, New York, New State Armory
Rutland, Vermont, Merchants Row
Sacramento, California, State Capitol

Salem, Massachusetts, Salem Witch
Salem Reform Church, Allentown, Pennsylvania, British Anchor, 1913
Spirit of 1776, No. 15. Ye Old Historical Pottery
Springfield, Illinois, State Capitol
Springfield, Massachusetts, Municipal Group
Springfield, Massachusetts, New Municipal Building
Syracuse, New York, Court House
Taunton, Massachusetts, Fountain on the Green
Topeka, Kansas, State Capitol
Valley Forge, Pennsylvania, Washington's Headquarters, 1777-78, dated 1910
Washington Crossing the Delaware, No. 7. Ye Old Historical Pottery
Washington State, Washington's Headquarters ?
Washington, D.C., Capitol, No. 8. Ye Olde Historical Pottery
White Mountains, New Hampshire, Old Man of the Mountain, R and M, Ye Olde Historical Blue Plate Co.
"Why Worry?" Sailor in Rocking Chair, Ye Olde Historical Pottery
Wilkes-Barre, Pennsylvania, Court House
Woonsocket, Rhode Island, U.S. Post Office
Yale, Old Brick Row, New Haven, Connecticut
Yale University, New Haven, Connecticut

Cups and saucers, all standard size—not demitasse

Albany, New York
Brooklyn, New York
Chicago, Illinois
Indianapolis, Indiana
Lenox, Massachusetts
Lewis and Clark Exposition
Minneapolis, Minnesota
New York, New York
Niagara Falls, New York
Panama-Pacific International Exposition, San Francisco, 1915
Philadelphia, Pennsylvania
Pittsburgh, Pennsylvania
Plymouth, Massachusetts
Portland Maine
Provincetown, Massachusetts
Put-In-Bay, Ohio, (brown) (green)
St. Louis, Missouri, World's Fair, 1904
Washington, D.C.
Williamsburg, Virginia
Yale

Tumblers—all about four inches tall

Albany, New York
Asheville, North Carolina

Fall River, Massachusetts
Halifax, Nova Scotia
Niagara Falls, New York
New London, Connecticut
Montreal, PQ (brown)
Plymouth, Massachusetts, 1906
Plymouth, Massachusetts, (slightly larger than first example)
Seattle
Tacoma, Washington, Royal Fenton mark
Thousand Islands
Washington, D.C. (green)

Hollowware and other miscellaneous items

Bread Plate, Plymouth, Coats of Arms of Mayflower Families, dated 1909 (multi-color)
Butter Pat, Plymouth, Massachusetts, Landing of the Pilgrims, 1620 (Burbank)
Fern Pot and Stand, Portraits of women by British artists
Pitchers, round, American Pilgrims, Pilgrim Plymouth, many colors and combinations, brown, green, grey-blue, blue-green, multicolor; tankard type pitcher, Discovery of America 1492, same colors as round pitchers
Platter, Plymouth in 1622, 13 by 16 inches (multicolor)
Salt and Pepper Shakers, Plymouth, MA, 4 scenes of Plymouth (Burbank)
Sugar and Creamer, Pilgrim Plymouth, American Pilgrims, Burbank, Ye Old Historical Pottery
Vases, The Countess Grosvenor, Mrs. Robinson, Mrs. Luddens, The World's Fair, St. Louis, Missouri, 1904, unknown number of different views, some have two handles and others have handle and spout

Odd Plates

Asbury Park, New Jersey, blue-grey, 8 3/4 inches
Delaware Water Gap, blue-grey, 8 3/4 inches
Crawford Cooking Ranges, advertising plate, creamer also known
Harrisburg, Pennsylvania, The New State Capitol ?
Mrs. Robinson by Sir Joshua Reynolds
Heart Island, Thousand Islands, blue-grey, 8 3/4 inches
University of Pennsylvania, unusual border
Yukon-Pacific Exposition, blue-grey, 8 3/4 inches

ROYAL CROWN STAFFORDSHIRE

TRENTHAM BONE CHINA LTD.
Longton Staffordshire, England
1952-1957

Queen Mary, souvenir from ship docked in California, 6 inches

ROYAL FENTON
England

This company is not listed in Godden or Chaffers. The firm was evidently in business during the early part of the twentieth century. The mark appears on some R. and M. imports which would definitely date it before 1939. Royal Fenton could have been a subsidiary of a larger company.

Coats of Arms of 13 original states, center has Great Seal of U.S., rolled edge, coats of arms in border, blue on grey, pat. 1908
Don't Give Up the Ship
Miles Standish Monument, Standish crest surrounded by six scenes, Longfellow poem on back, brown
Surrender of Col. William Ledyard, D.A.R. insignia at top, reverse **Massacre of Fort Griswold, Groton, Connecticut, Sept. 16, 1781**, issued by Anna Warner Bailey Chapter D.A.R. 1906, mauve, 10 inches
Valley Forge, 1777-1778, Washington's Headquarters, six border scenes, reverse **Desc. of Valley Forge**, by Cyrus E. Brady, copyright by Gus Golf, Dec. 19, 1910, amethyst

ROYAL STAFFORDSHIRE POTTERY
Arthur J. Wilkinson, Ltd.
Burslem Staffordshire, England
1885

The Wilkinson Pottery Company first used the Royal Staffordshire backstamp in 1907 and revived the mark in 1947 when it began making commemoratives for Jonroth.

Franconia Notch, New Hampshire, Cannon Mountain Tramway, in center, narrow border, blue, 6 7/8 inches
Moccasin Bend from Lookout Mountain, four border scenes, backstamped Jonroth, blue, 9 7/8 inches
Nashville, Capitol of Tennessee, Jonroth
Salem, Massachusetts, cup and saucer, blue; creamer, lavender
U.S. Capitol, Washington, bowl (early, pre-1920), blue, 9 1/2 inches
Virginia Building, Jamestown Exposition, 1907, 5 border scenes, deep blue, 10 1/2 inches

ROYAL WINTON

see Grimwades

ROYAL WORCESTER
Worcester Royal Porcelain Company, Ltd.
Worcester, England
1862-

Royal Worcester is not a name one would associate with souvenir ware. The company is best known for the Dorothy Doughty birds made from 1946 to 1960 and for fine porcelain dinner sets and ornamental objects. Many potteries hardly deserve the appendage "Royal" added to their name, but Worcester is the exception. The backstamp is "manufacturers to their majesties." From 1892 until 1965, the company used a peculiar system of dots, circles, and other devices to indicate dates. The table is interpreted in Godden's book of marks.

Andrew Jackson, First Governor of Florida
Old City Gates, St. Augustine, Florida, settled 1595, border has views of exclusive hotels, 1917, deep bright blue, 10 inches
Old Man of the Mountain, B.C. 2000, eagle and Indian in center, grape cluster and leaf border, 10 1/2 inches
Ponce De Leon, portrait in center, border same as first entry, dated 1912, blue 10 inches
St. Augustine, Florida

SARREGUEMINES
France

Lindbergh, "Lindy's" Portrait, dated 1927

SEBRING POTTERY COMPANY
Sebring, Ohio
1887-1940s

Lindbergh's First Flight, 1927, yellow, 8 1/2 inches

SHENANGO POTTERY
Trenton, New Jersey
1955-see Lamberton-Scammell

Alaska Railroad demi cup and saucer
Baltimore and Ohio, cup and saucer, train scenes
McMicken Hall, University of Cincinnati, 1930 (limited edition), 10 1/2 inches (does not fit in with date of establishment of pottery)
Ships Constitution and Guerriere, porcelain, pink, 10 1/2 inches

SIMPSON'S LTD
Ambassador Ware
Cobridge, Staffordshire, England
1944-

Ambassador Ware is a trade name used by Simpson's Limited. This company was incorporated in 1944 and was formerly the Soho Pottery, Inc. The one example found appears to be identical to a series made by British Anchor. Only the color is somewhat different. The plate is dark blue, almost black. According to Godden, the mark was still being used in 1959.

SPODE

(see COPELAND)

STERLING CHINA COMPANY
East Liverpool, Ohio
1890-1920

This short-lived firm made a dinner set decorated in blue (called Plymouth Pilgrims) between 1900 and 1910. The company also made plates commemorating the building of the Panama Canal.

Panama Canal, map, with calendar surround, deep blue, border, 1918
Panama Canal, map, with surround of presidents' heads including Taft, 1913
R.H. Kobusch Furniture and Carpet Company, St. Louis, Missouri, black center, bright blue and gold border, earthenware, 8 1/4 inches

STEUBENVILLE POTTERY COMPANY
Steubenville, Ohio
1879-1959

This was another of the many Ohio firms producing ironstone and semi-porcelain in the last years of the nineteenth century. The company used at least fourteen different marks.

Dieu Et Mon Droit (God and my Right Hand), backstamped sponsored by the Bundles for Britain, Inc., reg. with U.S. Dept. of State, no. 235, white with seal and gold lion, 9 inches
U.S.S. Baltimore
U.S.S. Maine, blue on white, gold flecked border, (marked SpCp. and Canton—a name the company used for its semi-porcelain)

STOKE
GRIMWADES, LTD
Staffordshire, England
1900-

The backstamp Stoke or Stoke on Trent was used by the firm of Grimwades, Ltd. around 1900 and also in the 1930s. The Stoke mark was originally used by J. Plant and Company of Stoke. It was taken over by Grimwades in 1900. The Grimwades works was still in operation in the 1960s.

King's Chapel, Boston, blue, 9 1/2 inches
White House, the, blue

41

SWINNERTON'S LTD.
Hanley Staffordshire, England
1906

This company seems not to have been involved in the commemorative business except for one item which was made in several colors and sizes.

Niagara Falls, c. 1950, light blue, brown, green, multi-color, 6 7/8 inches, 9 inches, and 10 inches (larger plates have six border scenes)

UPPER HANLEY POTTERY COMPANY, LTD.
Hanley and Cobridge Staffordshire, England
1895-1910

The Upper Hanley Pottery Company made earthenware which it called semi-porcelain. One can date the items as follows: Hanley, 1895-1902; Brownfield's Works, 1902-1910; Cobridge, Staffordshire Potteries, 1895-1910.

Bluenose, Yarmouth, Bar Harbor Ferry, blue, 10 inches
Crawford Cooking Ranges, pitcher, blue, 4 3/4 inches; (agents for this stove company also gave away a plate and platter with the words Crawford Cooking Ranges in large script across the front — these were blue on white)

VAN HEUSEN CHARLES COMPANY
Importers
Albany, New York
1900-1930?

This firm appears to have imported only plates with views of Albany and of the state of New York, both historical and contemporary. They were made from about 1900 until 1933 and are generally called the "Albany" series. There were 19 altogether. All but one were made by Wedgwood. All have the "farrara" bor-der, a floral type border consisting of small flowers such as forget-me-nots.

---

1. Protestant Dutch Church
2. Washington's Headquarters, Newburgh
3. Market Street
4. Schuyler's House on the Flats
5. Fort Frederick
6. North Pearl Street from Manden Lane
7. St. Peters
8. Albany Female Academy
9. North Pearl Street and North Dutch Church
10. State and Pearl Streets
11. Fort Cralo
12. Van Renssaelaer Manor House
13. Residence of Major General Philip Schuyler
14. ?
15. Albany from Van Renssaelaer's Island
16. New Capitol, Albany, (made by Ridgway)
17. Old Capitol, Albany
18. Surrender of Burgoyne
19. Vanderheyden Palace, Albany

VERNON KILNS
Vernon, California
1930-1955

This now defunct American firm made hundreds (maybe thousands) of views of historical and scenic spots in the United States. There is no way of knowing just exactly what and how many of anything was made as records seem to be non-existent, as usual. There were sets of states, famous personalities, authors, artists, Presidents, cities, and more. Plates were made to commemorate centennials, local lore, regional events, etc. They were made in two sizes, 8 1/2 and 10 1/2 inches. The colors are blue, green, pink, red, brown, black and possibly others. These plates can be found at almost any flea market but have not yet worked their way up to the legitimate antique shows. They could never be mistaken for English ware as the scenes are rather flat, not dimensional, and the colors are not intense. Most of the scenes look like line drawings. On some the effect is spoiled by the crowding in of too many scenes with no emphasis on any one thing. These plates do not seem to be attracting much attention from serious collectors, but eventually they probably will as some were designed by famous American artists such as Rockwell Kent. The list is only a small sampling of what is available.

Abraham Lincoln, wartime presidents series, brown, 10 1/2 inches
Albuquerque's 150th Anniversary
Belleville, Illinois, Courthouse, blue, 10 1/2 inches
Bit of the Old South, house on the river, a southern mansion, various colors, 8 1/2 inches
Evergreen State, blue on cream, 10 1/2 inches
Excelsior Springs, blue on cream, 10 1/2 inches
Georgia State Capitol, Atlanta
Historic St. Augustine, blue
Indiana, state of
Michigan, state of
Moby Dick, signed Rockwell Kent, blue, 8 1/2 inches
Mt. Rushmore Memorial, blue, 10 1/2 inches
New Hampshire
North Dakota, blue, 10 1/2 inches
Old Monterey, 10 1/2 inches
Picture Map of Old North Carolina
Presidents plate, Washington through Truman
Shawnee Creek Kilns, blue
Tri-Cities, blue, 10 1/2 inches
Van Wert, Ohio, courthouse, blue
Williams, Arizona

JOSIAH WEDGWOOD and SONS
formerly Etruria
since 1940, Barleston, England
1759-

If potteries were listed by importance and influence rather than in alphabetical order, Wedgwood would certainly be first on almost any list. The history of this old and respected firm can be found in any good book about the English ceramic industry. The Wedgwood Company made plates in several colors for the World's Columbian Exposition 1893 (see list). The collecting craze really got underway about 1895 when the Jones, McDuffee and Stratton Company of Boston ordered a series of plates to be made in the deep rich blue reminiscent of the pre-1830 Staffordshire which was even then being collected by antique enthusiasts of the time. The border was a full blown or cabbage rose design taken from an old Staffordshire pattern. Most of the views were of Boston and vicinity although there were others including a few of California missions. These blue plates were so popular, Jones, McDuffee and Stratton continued to import them until the mid-1960s when the company merged with another firm and discontinued the importation of commemoratives. An extensive list of these views has been compiled and published by Frank Stefano of Brooklyn, New York.

Several other firms also imported Wedgwood views. Two of the better known ones were Mellen and Hewes of Hartford, Connecticut and the Van Heusen Charles Company of Albany, New York.

To determine the age of a Wedgwood plate, one should refer to the impressed number rather than the copyright date. For example, a view of Old North Church is stamped copyright 1903 but the actual date of manufacturer is 1930. The following is a list of letters used from 1898 to 1930. Three letters are impressed. The third letter (on the right) indicates the actual year of manufacture.

A 1898	K 1908	V 1919
B 1899	L 1909	W 1920
C 1900	M 1910	X 1921
D 1901	N 1911	Y 1922
E 1902	O 1912	Z 1923
F 1903	P 1913	4A 1924
G 1904	Q 1914	4B 1925
H 1905	R 1915	4C 1926
I 1906	S 1916	4D 1927
J 1907	T 1917	4E 1928
	U 1918	4F 1929

From about 1907 the number "3" replaces the first letter. From 1924 the number "4" replaces the "3." From 1930 on, the last two numbers indicate the year and the first letter indicates the month. For example, A40 means January 1940.

The following views were made before 1910, the year Jones, McDuffee and Stratton celebrated its 100th anniversary. They are all blue and have the cabbage rose border. All are 9 1/4 inches in diameter.

Abraham Lincoln (portrait) 1907
Adjacent Leanto Houses
Alamo 1907
Alexandria Bay, New York, 1899
Arlington, Home of Martha Custis 1900
Athenaeum, Hartford, Connecticut 1904
Battle on Lexington Common 1900
Benton Harbor, Michigan, The City 1906
Birth of the American Flag
Birthplace of Longfellow, Portland, Maine
Birthplace of Whittier
Block Island, Rhode Island, Southeast Lighthouse 1902
Boston Common and Statehouse, 1896
Boston in 1776
Boston Tea Party
Boston Town House
Bunker Hill Monument 1907
California's Mission Hotel, 1903
Capitol, Washington, D.C., close up view 1908
Capitol, Washington, D.C., distant view 1903
Capitol Building, Albany, New York 1904
Capitol Building, Albany, New York early view 1901
Captain John Parker, Lexington 1898
Capture of Fort Ticonderoga 1905
Capture of Vincennes, 1901
Carpenter's Hall, Philadelphia 1901
Catedal De Aqua Scalkentes, Mexico 1905
Charles Bellows House, Walpole, New Hampshire 1909
Charter Oak, Hartford, Connecticut 1904
Chew House, Germantown, Pennsylvania 1902
City Hall, Waterville, Maine 1903
City Hall and Post Office, Hartford, Connecticut 1902
Colorado State Capitol
Dorothy Q. Mansion, birthplace Quincy, Massachusetts 1907
East Boston Bethel Church, 1907
Elmwood, Cambridge, Massachusetts, home of J.R. Lowell

Fairbanks Family
Faneuil Hall, Cradle of Liberty, 1742
Farragut House, Rye Beach, New Hampshire 1905
Fifth Avenue Hotel, Madison Square, New York 1903
First Church in Orrville, 1907
First Church, Quincy, Massachusetts 1903
First Congregational Church
First Ticonderoga Series
Fort Dearborn, Michigan 1902
Fort Johnson, Amsterdam, New York
Fresno City Court House, Fresno, California 1907
Frontenac Hotel 1907
Garfield Memorial 1901
George Washington, 1907
Glenwood Campenelle and Chimes 1903
Governor Langdon House, Portsmouth, New Hampshire 1907
Governor Wentworth Mansion, Portsmouth, New Hampshire 1902
Grand Council of NEUCT of America, Souvenir of 14th Annual Session 1907
Grace House in the Fields, New Canaan, Connecticut 1903
Grand Union Hotel, Saratoga Springs, New York, 1907
Grant's Tomb, Riverside on the Hudson 1901
Green Dragon Tavern
Grover Cleveland
Half Moon on the Hudson, 1909
Harvard College Gate 1899
Hermitage, Home of Andrew Jackson
Hetmere, Beverly, Massachusetts
Home of Caroline Scott Harrison
Home of Mary Livermore
Home of Ralph Waldo Emerson
Home of United Women's Efforts, Lynn, Massachusetts 1907
Hoosiac Tunnel, North Adams, Massachusetts 1898
Horseshoe Curve, Altoona, Pennsylvania 1901
Hotel Green, Pasadena, California 1903
Hotel Maryland, Pasadena, California 1904
Hotel Raymond, Pasadena, California 1903
House of Seven Gables, Salem, Massachusetts
Independence Hall, Philadelphia, 1893
In Memorial, Wm. McKinley, President of United States 1908
Interior of Christ Church, Philadelphia, Pennsylvania 1902
Jan Mabie House, Rotterdam, New York 1902
John Hancock House, Boston 1899
King's Chapel, Boston
Lamb Tavern, 1746, Boston
Landing of the Pilgrims 1903
Lee Mansion, Marblehead, Massachusetts 1909
Library of Congress, 1897

Lincoln's Home, Springfield, Illinois, 1902
Lighthouse Point, Lake Superior, Marquette, Michigan, 1905
Lockport, New York, 1909
Longfellow's Early Home, Portland, Maine
Longfellow's House, Cambridge, Massachusetts, 1848
Maine Capitol, built in 1829, enlarged in 1870, 1900
Maplewood Hotel, Pittsfield, Massachusetts 1900
Maplewood Hotel, Pittsfield, Massachusetts, small view, 1899
Martha Custis, Wife of George Washington
Massachusetts General Hospital, 1903
Mayflower Arriving in Provincetown Harbor
Mayflower in Plymouth Harbor, 1899
McKinley Home, Canton, Ohio, 1901
McKinley Monument, Buffalo, New York, 1907
Media Hotel and Mineral Baths, Mt. Clemens, Michigan, 1907
Memorial Continental Hall, Washington, D.C., built in 1905
Memorial Church, Stanford, University, Palo Alto, California, 1898
Michigan College of Mines, Houghton, Michigan, 1905
Minnehaha Falls, Minneapolis, Minnesota, 1900
Monticello, Home of Thomas Jefferson, 1902
Mormon Temple Block, 1901
Mount of the Holy Cross, 1901
Mount Vernon
Nantucket (windmill) 1746, 1899
Nathaniel Hawthorne, 1904
Nebraska State Capitol
New American, Massachusetts, 1901
New State Capitol, Harrisburg, Pennsylvania, 1900
Niagara Falls, 1901
Old Boston Theatre, 1899
Old Brick Church, Boston, 1898 (gold edge)
Old Capitol Building, Albany, New York, 1904
Old City Gateway, St. Augustine, Florida, 1903
Old Corner Bookstore, Boston, 1901
Old Feather Store, Boston, 1898
Old First Congregational Church, Chicago, Illinois, 1909
Old Ironsides
Old Man of the Mountain, New Hampshire (distant view), 1900
Old Man of the Mountain, New Hampshire (close up view)
Old Meeting House, Hingham, Massachusetts, 1905
Old Nathan Hale School House, 1901
Old North Bridge, Concord, Mass.
Old North Church, Salem Street, Boston
Old South Church, Boston, 1898

Old State House, Boston, 1890 built in 1657, 1894
Old State House, East End, Boston, 1899
Old Stone Mill, Newport, Rhode Island
Old Sun Tavern, Faneuil Hall Square, Boston, 1900
Old Town Church, ME., Oldest Bell Tower in America, 1901
Old Town Mill, New London, Connecticut, 1900
Old Windmill, Nantucket Island, 1907
Orr Docks, Escanaba, Michigan, 1905
Park Hotel and Baths, Mt. Clemens, Michigan, 1907
Park Street Church, Boston, 1904
Paul Revere's Ride, 1907
Pearl of Orr's Island, 1903
People's Church, Bethal, Maine, 1908
Picturesque Santa Barbara, Hotel Potter, 1909
Pike's Peak from Garden of the Gods
Pilgrim Exiles, 1903
Pilgrim Memorial, Provincetown, Massachusetts
Pilgrim Memorial Monument, Old Rear View, 1906
Plymouth, Massachusetts, the Harbor 1622, 1904
Poe Lock, Sault Ste. Marie, Michigan, 1903
Poland Spring, Maine, 1900
Priscilla and John Alden
Public Library, Boston, 1895
Quincy Homestead, Massachusetts, 1894
Rear View of Independence Hall, Philadelphia, 1908
Red Lion Inn, In the Berkshires, Stockbridge, Massachusetts, 1902
Return of the Mayflower
Riverside, California, County Courthouse, 1904
St. Augustine, Florida, 1904
St. Anne By the Sea, Kennebunkport, Maine, 1906
St. Michael's Church, Loretto, Pennsylvania, 1903
St. Stephen's Church, Portland, Maine, 1896
San Carlos DeMonterey or Carmel Mission, 1898
San Fernando Mission, Los Angeles County, California, 1903
San Gabriel Archangel Mission, California (without bells), 1901
San Gabriel Archangel Mission, California (with bells), 1909
San Juan, Capistrano, California, 1906
San Luis Rey, DeFrancia Mission, California, 1899
Sankoty Head Light, Nantucket, 1907
Santa Barbara (California) Mission
Saratoga Battle Monument, 1907

Saratoga Battle Monument (close view), 1903
Sibley House
Signing of the Declaration of Independence, 1900
Smith College, Northhampton, Massachusetts, 1904
Soldier's Memorial Arch, Hartford, Connecticut, 1904
Spirit of '76, "Yankee Doodle"
Springfield, Illinois, State Capitol, 1901
State Capitol, Hartford, Connecticut, 1909
State Flower series
State House, Boston
State House, Boston, Ded. July 4, 1785, Bulfinch Arch, 1901
State Street and Old State House, Boston
Stevens Institute of Technology, Hoboken, New Jersey, 1900
Summit House, Mt. Tom, 1909
Summit House, Mt. Tom Before the Fire, 1899
Surrender of Burgoyne
Theodore Roosevelt
Trinity Church, Copley Square, Boston
Trinity College, Hartford, Connecticut, 1901
Ulysses S. Grant portrait, 1899
Union Station, Washington, D.C., 1906
United States Frigate "Constitution" in Chase, 1903
United States Naval Academy
Upper Falls, Rumford Falls, Maine, 1905
Van Alstine House, Canajoharie, New York, 1899
Warner House, Portsmouth, New Hampshire, 1902
Washington Crossing the Delaware, 1899
Washington Elm, Cambridge, Massachusetts
Washington Monument, Washington, D.C., 1895
Washington's Headquarters, Newburgh, New York, 1899
Washington's Headquarters, Newburgh, New York (close up rear), 1901
Washington's Headquarters, Newburgh, New York (without pole,rear), 1903
Washington's Headquarters, Newburgh, New York (with pole), 1909
Webb House, Wethersfield, Connecticut, 1907
Wellesley College
Wendell Hotel, Pittsfield, Massachusetts, 1904
West Point series
White House, Washington, D.C.
Women's Christian Temperance Union (W.C.T.U.), 1908
Yale College and Old Yale Fence

Additional Wedgwood views

Abbot Academy, Andover, Massachusetts
Abbot Academy Centennial, 1929
Abraham Lincoln portrait, acorn and leaf border, brown, 8 1/2 inches
Abraham Lincoln, border scenes, (made for *Register and Leader*, Des Moines, Iowa), blue 10 inches
Agnes Scott College, Buttrick Hall
Aiken Homestead, Norwich, Connecticut
Akron Women's Club, Akron, Ohio
Alabama State Capitol, Montgomery; blue, 1944; rose, 1951, 9 3/4 inches
Alamo, the, sponsored by the Fort Worth D.A.R., 1936, blue, 10 1/2 inches
Albany views (see Van Hoesen Charles and Co.)
Alexandria Bay, New York
Alexandria Bay, Heart Island
Altoona, Pennsylvania, Horseshoe Curve
American Eagle, eagle is brown, has red, white, blue shield on breast, white stars on blue ground, red, white and blue border
American Historical Scenes, blue with gold edge (slight greenish tinge) set of six, 1900, 9 inches
American Sailing Ships, 1950; Somers, Columbus, Mayflower, Oakley, Curtes, Bethal
American West, first edition, 1939, cream with blue center scene, (border is raised design with symbols of the West), 10 3/4 inches
Amsterdam, New York
    Fort Jackson
    Guy Park
Anthers, Colorado Springs, Colorado
Anthony Wayne, superimposed on old fort, bramble border, blue, 10 inches
Arkansas Statehood Centennial, 1936
Arkansas, 1951, blue, 10 1/2 inches
Augusta, Maine, World War I Memorial
(Mary) Baldwin College, Administration Building
Bennington Battle Monument, 1947
Benton Harbor, Michigan
Berry School, Mount Berry Chapel, Mt. Berry, Georgia
Birthplace of Dorothy Q Mansion, Quincy, Massachusetts, blue, 9 1/2 inches
Blue Mountain College, 75th Anniversary
"Bore," the Petocodiac River, Monkton, New Brunswick
Boston Purple with Johnny Appleseed, bramble border, 1967, rose pink, 10 inches
Boston Repertory Theatre, 1927
Boston Tea Party, 1951, blue, 10 1/4 inches
Boston University, 1948
Branford, Connecticut, the Russell House
Bridgeport, Connecticut, the Centennial, 1936
Bunker Hill Monument (2 views)
California Missions, dated before 1885, blue, 8 inches, cut corners; since 1932, in blue and three other color combinations, 8 and 10 inches
California Republic 1939
    Donner Expedition 1846
    Finding of Gold by James Marshall 1848
    Los Angeles 1854

First Admission Day, San Francisco 1850
Overland Mail Stage Station, San Luis
Obispo 1875
San Carlos Mission 1770
Sutter's Fort 1848
Raising the Flag at Monterey 1846
San Francisco 1846
Golden Hind, Sir Francis Drake 1579
Fremont Crosses the Sierra 1844
Landing of Cabrillo, Discovering San
Diego 1542
Campus Martius, Marietta, Ohio, 1938, blue
Canada, Crown, bright colors, maple leaves,
1926, 10 inches
Captain Van Couver portrait, red and blue border, 10 inches
Capture of British Frigate, blue, 10 1/2 inches
Cedar Crest College, Administration Building
Chalfant House, Alleghany, Pennsylvania
**Champaign Memorial Monument, Plattsburg,
New York**
Charleston, South Carolina
Charter Oak, the, (imported by Mellen and
Hewes), blue
Chatham, Virginia, Chatham Hall
**Clark (George Rogers) Memorial, Vincennes,
Indiana**, 1931
Clark University 1837-1937
College of the Holy Cross, Alumni Hall
Col. William Prescott Homestead, blue
**Columbia College, Administration Building,
Columbia, South Carolina**
Columbian Exposition Series 1893
    1. Administration Building, black, 8
    inches
    2. Agricultural Building, black, 8 inches;
    brown, 8 1/2 inches
    3. Electrical Building, pink, brown, 8 1/2
    inches
    4. Horticultural Building, black, 8 inches;
    brown, 8 1/2 inches; black, 9 1/2
    inches with scalloped edge
    5. Machinery Hall, 8 1/2 inches
    6. U.S. Government Building, black, blue,
    8 1/2 inches
Coolidge Homestead, tile, 1925, brown
**Concord, Massachusetts, First Parish Church
1636-1951**
**Concord, Massachusetts, Home of Ralph
Waldo Emerson** (two views)
**Concord, Massachusetts, The Old North
Bridge**
Converse College, Spartanburg, South Carolina
Cuyahoga County Soldiers & Sailors Monument, Cleveland, Ohio
Dartmouth College
Davidson College 1837-1937
**Earlham College, Earlham Hall, Richmond,
Indiana**, 1934

**Easton, Maryland, Old Third Haven Meeting
House**
Ellsworth Homestead, Windsor, Connecticut,
D.A.R. 1929
Erie Public Library (3)
Evangeline, "Wives were Parted," 1902, blue,
10 1/2 inches
Exeter Academy, 1780-1856, Wedgwood Society, set of four
Faneuil Hall, bluebell border, 1929
Federal City, series of four, made for Chas.
Schwartz and Son, Washington, D.C., bone
china, black and white, flag and eagle and
cherry blossom border
    The White House
    The Capitol
    Panorama of Washington Monument,
    Lincoln Memorial, and the Capitol
**Fenimore Hall, N.Y.S.H.A., Cooperstown, New
York**
First Federalist Church, Georgia, roses border
Fisher Junior College, Boston
Florida State University, Westcott Building
Fort Dearborn (1893 exposition?), blue, 9
inches, black center
Fort Johnson, Amsterdam, New York, 1942,
blue
Fort Ticonderoga on Lake Champlain
**Fort Ticonderoga, the South Barracks, 1775-
1955**, deep maroon, floral border, 9 1/2 inches
Fort Ticonderoga, Bicentennial, 1955, blue, 9
1/2 inches
Fort Ticonderoga, Winter Scenes
**Framingham Academy, Library Building,
Framingham, Massachusetts**, blue
Framingham Academy library, 1900
Fredericksburg, Virginia, Kenmore
French Trinity Church, Boston, deep blue, 10
inches
Furman University, Bell Tower
Garden Club of America
    English 18th Century
    Spanish
    Early Italian
    Flemish
    French
    England
    Chinese
    Japanese
    Persian
    Egyptian
    Mount Vernon
    Williamsburg
**Gardner Massachusetts, Elisha Jackson House
1765-1935**
Governor's Palace, Williamsburg, Virginia,
black, 1953, multi-color, 1955, 10 1/2 inches
Grand Council of New England, roses border
Grant's Tomb, Riverside Drive, New York (3
views)

Great Stone Face, tile, blue, in black frame

Greenboro Lodge, 125th Anniversary, 1946, Greenboro, North Carolina

Greenboro Masonic & Eastern Star Home, 1950, Greenboro, North Carolina

Guildford College, 1837-1937, Founders Hall

Hamden, Connecticut, The Old Red House

Hannah Fuston Monument, tile, Haverhill, Massachusetts,(green) 3 1/4 by 4 5/8 inches

Harrisburg, Pennsylvania, The New State Capitol

Harrison and Tecumseh, blue, 9 1/4 inches

Hartford, Connecticut, state capitol, blue, 9 inches

Harrison, William Henry, Centennial, 1941

Harrison Mansion, Vincennes, Indiana

Hartford, Connecticut

Hendrick Hudson, Half Moon, tea set, Washington Inauguration sesquicentennial, 1789-1932, embossed ship, white on cobalt, spread eagle and arrow on reverse

Hermitage Mansion, Home of Andrew Jackson, blue, 1962, 10 3/4 inches

High Rock Springs, Saratoga Springs, New York

Hill School, 1936, Alumni Hall

Historical Homes, by Isabel Marshall, 1927, set of twelve, 9 inches

Home of Cornet Joseph Parsons, ferrara border

Home of the United Women's Efforts, (Lynn Women's Clubhouse)

Home of Washington, Mt. Vernon, insets of George and Martha, (imported by George Bowman Company)

Home of Whittier

Hoosac Tunnel, North Adams, Massachusetts

Horseshoe Curve, Altoona, Pennsylvania

Howard College, Birmingham, Alabama, Old Main

Huntington College, Flowers Hall, Centennial, 1954

Illinois College, Beecher Hall, Jacksonville, Illinois, 1952, 125th anniversary, white floral embossed border, blue scene in center, 10 3/4 inches

Indian Hunter Menotomy, Arlington, Massachusetts

Indiana, First State Capitol

Indiana University, Memorial Hall

Indians of High Rock Springs, New York, Indians in center, border shows Saratoga scenes, blue, 10 inches

Institute of Technology, Boston, sepia, 7 inches

In the Berkshires, Red Lion Inn, Stockbridge, Massachusetts

Iroquois Sally Winter, Grand Champion Female, National Dairy Show, 1929

Jorden Marsh Centennial Plates 1951
  Faneuil Hall

Battle of Concord Bridge
Old State House
Battle of Bunker Hill
Boston Tea Party
Action Between Constitution and Guerrierre

Long Island, floral border, sepia, 10 1/2 inches

John Patterson (a ship?) Hamilton, Ontario, rolled edge, blue, 10 inches

John Quincy Adams House, Quincy, Massachusetts, brown

John Stark and Ethan Allen, deep blue, 10 inches

Kansas Shawnee Mission Centennial 1937

Kenmore, Home of Betty Lewis

Kent State Administration Building, blue, 10 1/4 inches

King's Chapel, bluebell border, blue, 1948, 10 1/4 inches

LaGrange College, Georgia, Smith Hall

Lake George, Monument Commemorating Battle of 1755

Langdon House, Portsmouth, New Hampshire

Lee Mansion, Marblehead, Massachusetts

Lighthouse Point, Lake Superior, Marquette, Michigan

Lincoln Memorial, Lincoln standing in center, border scenes, blue, 10 inches

Lincoln bust, roses border, gold edge, blue, 1907, 9 inches

Lockport, New York

Long Island Tercentenary, 1936

Long Meadow, Massachusetts

Longfellow, portrait in center, verses in border, blue, 9 inches (pre J. Mc. and S.)

Longfellow House, 1785, six border scenes, blue, 9 3/4 inches

Longfellow Series
  Song of Hiawatha
  Paul Revere's Ride
  The Children's Hour
  The Village Blacksmith
  Courtship of Miles Standish
  Evangeline

Loretto, Pennsylvania, St. Michael's Church

(Jan) Mabie House, Rotterdam, New York

MacMurray College, Jacksonville, Illinois, 1946, Main Hall

Madison College, Harrisonburg, Virginia, Wilson Hall

Maine Capitol, Augusta, Maine

Maine Capitol, 1899, 250th anniversary of incorporation, 1649-1899, three seals and three scenes in shell, wreath, and garland border, blue, 10 1/2 inches

Manchester in the Mountains, Vermont

Marietta College, Erwin Hall

Maryland College for Women, 1935

Massachusetts General Hospital Building, deep blue

Massachusetts Charitable Eye and Ear Infirmary, 1850-1899

McKinley Monument, Buffalo, New York

Marblehead, Massachusetts

Massacre of Fort Griswold, Groton, Connecticut, 1781, deep blue, 10 inches

Mayflower Commemorative, 1970, brown, 10 1/2 inches

Medea Hotel & Mineral Baths, Mt. Clemens, Michigan

Medical College of Virginia, 1938, Egyptian Building

Melrose Public Library, Melrose, Massachusetts

Memorial Continental Hall, D.C. (D.A.R.)

Mendota, Minnesota, The Sibley House (D.A.R.)

Memorial Hall, Framingham, Massachusetts, 10 inches

Merit Hall, 1939, 10 inches

Michigan College of Mines, Houghton, Michigan

Middlebury, Vermont, Congregational Church

Milton, Massachusetts, 250th Anniversary

Minnehaha Falls, Minnesota

Mission Hotel, Riverside, California, blue, roses border, 9 1/4 inches

Montgomery Historical Society, Amsterdam, New York, blue

Monticello, maroon, 10 inches

Monticello, Home of Thomas Jefferson, pink

Monument Over Plymouth Rock, old house in background, blue

Moorings (the), Hampton, Virginia, 1929

Morman Temple Block, Salt Lake City

Mount Mansfield, roses border

Mount of the Holy Cross, Colorado

Mount Tom, Summit House (Mount Tom Railway)

Mount Washington from Intervale, NH

Muldoon, Massachusetts, 1899

Nantucket

Nantucket Island, Old Coffee House (Ferrara border)

Nantucket Island, Old Windmill (Ferrara border)

Nantucket Island, Sankoty Light Head (Ferrara border)

Nashville, Tennessee, Hermitage Mansion

Natchez on the Mississippi

Nebraska State Capitol, Lincoln

New Albany, Indiana, Scribner House

New American, Pittfield, Massachusetts

New Canaan, Connecticut, Grace House in the Fields

New-Castle-on-the-Delaware, Read House, 1801

New Harmony, Indiana, Old Fauntleroy House

New Jersey Church Series
St. Johns Church-Salem 1722
St. Peters Church-Spotswood 1756
Trinity Cathedral-Newark 1745
Christ Church-Middletown 1702
St. Peters Church-Freehold 1702-1736
St. Peters Church-Clarksboro 1765-1770
St. James Church-Piscataway 1705
Christ Church-Newton 1769
Christ Church-New Brunswick 1742
Christ Church-Shrewsbury 1702
St. Peters Church-Perth Amboy
St. Marys Church-Burlington 1702
St. Johns Church-Elizabeth 1702

New London, Connecticut, Old Town Mill

Newport, Rhode Island, The Old Stone Mill

New York Fifth Avenue Hotel, Madison Square

Newark Art Club 1929
Newark Art Club
Trinity Cathedral
Cathedral of the Sacred Heart
Court House and Lincoln Statue
Old Center Market
First Presbyterian Church
Industrial Newark
The Library
House of Prayer
Newark Academy
Museum
Mutual Benefit Life Insurance

New York World's Fair, set of 12, all backstamped, Inauguration of George Washington, 1789, World's Fair, 1939, oak leaf border, maroon, 10 1/2 inches

New York World's Fair, series, "First Edition," only 500 made, 12 in set, sold by Macy's Dept. Store, New York City, brochure and container included, blue, 10 inches

Niagara Falls

Northeast Missouri State Teachers College, John R. Kirk Memorial

Old Avery Homestead, Groton, Connecticut, bowl, 2 1/2 by 4 1/2 inches

Old Boston Post Office, blue, 10 inches

Old Fauntleroy Home, blue, 9 inches

Old First Congregational Church, Chicago

Old Flume and Stairs, Franconia Notch, pre-1885, octagonal shape plate, blue, 9 inches

Old Hubbard Tavern, Barleston mark-post 1940, 10 1/2 inches

Old Man of the Mountain, pre-1885, octagonal shape plate, blue, 8 inches; floral border, 7 inches; flower border, 8 1/2 inches; octagonal, green; cup and saucer, blue; plate, blue, 6 inches; miniature pitcher, sepia; six-sided pitcher, circa 1874, blue

Old Nathan Hale School House, Built 1774

Old North Church, bluebell border, 1930

Old State House, Boston, 1951, blue, 10 1/4 inches

Old Town Church, Oldest Bell Tower in America

Old Whale Ship, Gen. Williams
Oliver, Rebecca B. and David B., 1879-1936
Onata Lake, Pittsfield, Massachusetts
Ore Docks, Escanaba, Michigan
Orrville, First Church in Pautucket, Rhode Island, Congregational Church, 1839-1939, mulberry, 10 inches
Paoli, Indiana, Orange County Court House, D.A.R. 1935
Park Hotel & Baths, Clemens, Michigan
Parker, Captain John, Battle Green, Lexington
Parson, Cornet Joseph, home of, Northhampton, Massachusetts
Pasadena, California, Hotel Green
Pasadena, California, Hotel Raymond
Pasadena, California, Maryland, Hotel
Payne Memorial, "Home Sweet Home" East Hampton, New York
Peabody Museum, Salem, Massachusetts, 1949, views of ships
    Baltic
    Cleopatra's Barge
    Ulysses
    Essex
    Monk
    Grand Turk Highlander
    America
    Cruger
    Olinda Sooloo
    Margaret
Pearl (the) of Orr's Island, H. Beecher Stowe Story
Philadelphia State House
Pilgrim Memorial Monument, 1930
Pittsburgh, Pennsylvania, Cloverly, Dallas Avenue, 1886-1926
Pittsburgh, Pennsylvania, Holmhurst, 1922
Plumb's Maplewood Hotel, Pittsfield, Massachusetts
Poe Lock, Sault Ste. Marie, Michigan
Polytech Institute of Brooklyn, New York, Rogers Hall
Poland Springs
Portland Series, marked WMW Co., Portland, Maine
    City Hall 1919
    First Parish Church 1718
    Fort Georges, Portland Harbor
    Longfellow House
    Neal Dow House 1829
    Portland Headlight 1790
    Riverton Park 1896
Post Office, First Convention, 1904, sites in Massachusetts, blue, 10 inches
Prescott, Colonel William, Homestead, Pepperell, MA
Principia College, 1898-1947, The Chapel
Protestant Dutch Church, ferrara border
Railway Clerks 1904 Railway Post Office Clerks Convention

Randolph-Macon College, Ashland, Virginia, The Chapel
Repertory Theatre of Boston, the, made in 1927 to commemorate their 400th week, oak leaf border, mulberry, 10 1/2 inches
Red Lion Inn, Stockbridge, Massachusetts, deep blue, 9 1/2 inches
Ripon Wisconsin, First Congregational Church
Rhode Island Tercentenary, center anchor with state of Rhode Island above and "Hope" beneath, 1636-1937, limited first edition, made for Tilden-Thurber, Providence, blue, 10 inches
Rockland, Maine, Owl's Head
Rollens College
Robert E. Lee, home of, pink, 10 inches
Rosalie, Mississippi, Historic State Shrine, D.A.R.
Ruins of Old Spanish Mission, New Smyrna, Florida, 1930, blue, 9 3/4 inches
Rye Beach, New Hampshire, Farragut House
(Russell) Sage College 1916-1941, Gurley Hall
St. Ann's By the Sea
St. Augustine, Florida, Old City Gateway
St. Augustine, Florida, Tower of Fort San Marco
St. Lawrence Hotel, Columbia
St. Lawrence Seaway
St. Louis University, 1968
St. Mary's School and Junior College, Raleigh, North Carolina
St. Paul's, 1941, first edition
St. Paul's School, 1932, rose, 10 1/2 inches
St. Peter's Church, Clarksboro, blue, 9 inches
St. Polycarp's Church, Sommerville, Massachusetts

Sanctuary	Altar of the Sacred Heart
The Crib	Altar of the Blessed Virgin
The Repository	Sanctuary, Lower Church
The Rectory	School
The Convent	

Salisbury, North Carolina, St. John's Lutheran Church, 1953
San Juan, California Mission, blue, 9 1/4 inches
Sankoty Lighthouse, ferrara border
Saratoga Springs, New York, 1902, Indians and scenes of Saratoga Springs, blue, 10 inches (1903)
Schofield House, Indiana's Masonic Shrine, Madison, Indiana
Schyler House, bluebell border, blue
Scribner House, New Albany, Indiana
Seal of the Society of the D.A.R., queensware, issued by the National Society of the D.A.R., 1952, blue, 11 1/2 inches
Series of Sailing Ships

Ann McKim	Witch of the Waves
Stag Hound	Nightingale

50

Challenge	Sovereign of the Seas
N.B. Palmer	Young America
Witchcraft	Flying Cloud
Game Cock	Red jacket

Shaw Mansion, New London, Connecticut, 1902, deep blue

Shawnee Mission, Kansas (school for Indians)

Sibley House, Mendota, Minnesota, D.A.R.

Sibley House, Centennial of, D.A.R.

Site of Adams House, 1845, 9 inches

Skelton, Home of Doctor Henry, Southington, Connecticut

Snow Camp, North Carolina, Cave Creek Friends Church, 1751-1951

Southern Methodist University, Dallas Hall

Societas of Cincinnaterum (emblem) blue, 9 1/2 inches

Stanford University, 1935, blue, set of six, 10 inches, green; set of twelve, 10 inches

State Capitol Hartford, Connecticut (imported by Mellen and Hewes), blue

State House, Boston

State Normal School, Mary Hall, 1838-1939, Framingham, Massachusetts

State Teachers College, Bloomsburg, Pennsylvania

State Teachers College, Fainville, Virginia

Stevens Institute of Technology, Hoboken, New Jersey

Stone Mountain, Georgia, scalloped edge, black

Stockbridge, Massachusetts, Mission House 1739

Stratford Hall, Westmoreland Co., Virginia, Birthplace of Richard Henry Lee

Sunderland, Massachusetts, The Old Hubbard Tavern

Sunny Meadows Farm, Melvin Village, New Hampshire, 1932

Surrender of Col. Ledyard, made for D.A.R., 1908

Sweet Briar College, Sweet Briar House

Templeton, Massachusetts, John W. Stiles, Trader House, 1810

Texas

Texas Christian University 1873-1948

Tomochchi and his Companions, 1734, border has different states scenes, maroon, 10 1/4 inches

Town of Framingham, blue, 10 inches
1. Library Building and Framingham Academy, Inc., 1907
2. Memorial Hall and Academy, border has seals etc. Trinity
Transylvania Club
Burning of the Yazoo Act
John Wesley Teaching the Indians
Portraits of Great Georgians

Trinity Church, Boston, floral border, blue, 9 and 9 1/2 inches

Union Station, Washington, D.C.

United Commercial Travelers 14th Session Boston, 1908

U.S. Frigate "Constitution" 1960

University of Michigan, Women's League building, 1928

University of North Carolina, Main Entrance, Alumni Hall

University of Oklahoma, Administration Building

University of Richmond The Tower, West Hampton College

Universalist Church, Charleston, 9 inches

Upper Falls, Rumford Falls, Maine

Upper Iowa University, College Hall 1940

Van Alstyne House, Canajoharie, New York

Vanderheyden Mansion, ferrara border

Van Corlandt House, Colonial Dames of New York

Virginia Female Institute, Old Main and Stuart Hall

Waltham Watch Factory

Waltham Watch Factory, views, (eagle holding watch in claw), blue, 1904, 8 1/2, 8 3/4, 10 1/2 inches

Warner House, Portsmouth, New Hampshire

Washington Bi-Centennial 1932
Old Ironsides in Chase
Memorial Continental Hall
Birth of the American Flag
Independence Hall
Constitution Hall
Mount Vernon
Washington Monument
George Washington Portrait
Martha Washington Portrait
Surrender of Cornwallis
Signing of the Declaration of Independence
Seal of the D.A.R. Society

Washington, D.C., The Capitol

Washington, D.C., First Congregational Church, 10th & G, NW

Washington, D.C., National Gallery of Art

Washington, D.C., Union Station

Washington, D.C., Washington Monument

Washington, D.C., The White House

Watch tower Of Fort Marion, St. Augustine, Florida, blue

Waterbury, Connecticut, Home of A.S. Chase

Waterville, Maine, City Hall, built in 1902

Webb House, Wethersfield, Connecticut, D.A.R.

Wellesley College scenes, green on cream, 10 1/2 inches

Wells Commemorative Plate, 1863-1943

Wells Fargo Coach, Wells Commemorative Plate, 1868-1950

Wendell Hotel, Pittsfield, Massachusetts

Wentworth Mansion, Portsmouth, New Hampshire

Western College, Oxford, Ohio

Wheaton College, Wheaton, Illinois
Whittier, John Greenleaf, portrait, green, lines from three poems in border
William Henry Harrison Centennial, pink
Winchester, Virginia, First Congregational Church, 100th Anniversary 1940
Wiona State Teachers College, Somsen Hall, Wiona, Minnesota
Witch House, Also Known as Roger Williams House, 1634
Wittenburg College, pink
Woodrow Wilson Birthplace, Staunton, Virginia
Worcester, Massachusetts, Union Congregational Church
World Columbian Exposition, (see Columbian Exposition series)
World War Memorial, blue, 9 1/2 inches (Augusta, Maine)
Yale College and the Old Yale Fence
Yarmouth, Massachusetts, Old Meeting House

College Plate Series

Alabama College-4 views
Albion College-after 1949-3 views
Amherst College-12 views
Bates College 1939-2 views
Baylor University-after 1947-5 views
Boston University 1948-4 views
Bowdoin College 1931-7 views
Brenau College-4 views
Brown University-4 views
Bryn Mawr-12 views
Capitol University, Columbus, Ohio-1950-2 views
Coker College-2 views
Colby College, Waterville, Maine-8 views
Colby Junior College-3 views
City College of New York-12 views
College of the Holy Cross 1932-12 views
College of Notre Dame of Maryland-2 views
College of Our Lady of the Elms 1952-3 views
Columbia Plates, the 1932-12 views
Cornell University 1933-12 views
Denison University Centennial 1931-13 views (rose or purple)
Denison University one or a set made in 1955
Dickinson College-4 views
Duke University 1937-12 views
Elmore College-2 views
Emmanuel College-2 views
Fairleigh-Dickinson-3 views
Foxcroft 1934-6 views
Friends University, Wichita, KS 1936-2 views
Gettysburg College 1932-4 views
Greenboro College-3 views
Groton School 1935-4 views

Harvard University 1932-12 views, a dinner set consisting of 12 dinner plates, 12 lunch plates, cups and saucers, sugar and creamer, possibly more
Harvard University 1936 Tercentenary demitasse cups, 12 views (plates)
Harvard University 1941-14 views (red)
Heidelberg College 1950-4 views
Hollins College-4 views
Judson College-3 views
Limestone College 1945-3 views
Louisiana Polytechnic Institute-3 views
Massachusetts Institute of Technology 1930-12 views
Mercersburg Academy-12 views
Middlebury College-12 views
Mount Holyoke College-after 1938-15 views
New York University-12 views
Ohio University-7 views
Ohio Wesleyan University 1942-2 views
Pomona College-8 views
Princeton University 1930-12 views
Radcliff College-2 views
Randolph-Macon Women's College-2 views
Regis College-2 views
St. Lawrence University-after 1931-4 views
St. Marks School-4 views
St. Mary-of-the-Woods College-5 views
St. Paul's School-1928-12 views
Salem Academy-8 views
Smith College-1932-12 views
State Teachers College, Fernville, Virginia-2 views
Swarthmore College-6 views
Tamassee DAR School-6 views (also cups and saucers)
Trinity College, Hartford-4 views
Trinity College, Washington, D.C.-4 views
Tufts College 1932-4 views
Tulane University-4 views
Union College-4 views
U.S. Military Academy 1931?
U.S. Military Academy 1933-12 views (blue and rose)
U.S. Naval Academy 1935-12 views
University of California-Berkeley Campus-1932-12 views
University of California Diamond Jubilee-12 views cups and saucers
University of California Centennial 1968-12 views
University of Delaware-4 views
University of Georgia-6 views
University of Iowa 1935-12 views
University of Maine 1940-10 views
University of Michigan, 1926, 12 views
University of Michigan 1928?
University of Michigan 1935-13 views

University of Pennsylvania 1929-12 views
University of Pennsylvania 1940-12 views
University of Rochester-4 views
University of Southern California 1933-12 views
University of Texas-12 views
University of Virginia-12 views
University of Virginia, first edition, 1926-10 views, maroon
University of Seattle, Washington-4 views
Vassar College 1929-14 views
Virginia Military Institute-12 views
Wake Forrest College-after 1935-12 views
Washington and Lee-8 views
Wellesley College 1936-13 views
Wesleyan College 1936-3 views
Wesleyan University, Middletown, Connecticut 1931-12 views
Westtown School 1935-12 views
Wheaton College 1932-4 views
Emma Willard School-4 views
Williams College-12 views
Yale University-after 1931-13 views
Yale University 1949-6 views

The calendar tiles run from 1881 to 1929. They were made in various colors; blue, green, sepia and black.

1881 **Washington Headquarters, Cambridge**
1882 **Washington Statue, Public Gardens**
1883 **Ribbon Badge**
1884 (no view)
1885 **Map of Boston, 1772**
1886 **Portland Vase**
1887 **SS "Britannia" and SS "Etruria"**
1888 **Josiah Wedgwood's Portrait**
1889 **Faneuil Hall**
1890 **Old State House**
1891 **Adams Lean-to Houses, Quincy**
1892 **Mount Vernon**
1883 **Independence Hall, Philadelphia**
1894 **Boston Public Library**
1895 **State House, Boston**
1896 **Trinity Church, Boston**
1897 **Old Federal Street theatre**
1898 **King's Chapel**
1899 **Washington Elm**
1900 **John Hancock House**
1901 **Bunker Hill Monument**
1902 **Old North Church**
1903 **Elmwood, Home of James Russell Lowell**
1904 **United States Frigate "Constitution" in Chase**
1905 **The Stephenson and Twentieth Century Locomotives**
1906 **Jones, McDuffee and Stratton Co. Store, Franklin Street**
1907 **Harvard Stadium**
1908 **Harvard Medical School**

1909 **Boston Art Museum**
1910 **"Mayflower" Approaching Land**
1911 **U.S. Frigate "Constitution" and Battleship "Florida"**
1912 **Cunard Line Dock** (new), **Boston**
1913 **Pier 46 Mystic Wharves**
1914 **Pier Head of Commonwealth Dock, Boston**
1915 **Boston Custom House**
1916 **M.I.T.**
1917 **U.S. Navy Yard, Boston**
1918 **Boston Light**
1919 **Memorial Hall, Harvard University**
1920 **"Mayflower" in Plymouth Harbor, 1620**
1921 **John Harvard, Founder of Harvard College** (statue)
1922 **Cathedral Church of St. Paul**
1923 **Minute Man, Concord**
1924 **The Appeal of the Great Spirit**
1925 **The Flying Cloud** (a ship)
1926 **Coolidge Homestead**
1927 **Cathedral Church of St. Paul**
1928 **Plymouth Rock**
1929 **House of the Seven Gables**

Wedgwood tiles, six inches-square

Bunker Hill Monument 1900
Homestead of Fairbanks Family in America 1904
Lee Mansion, Marblehead, Massachusetts
Lynn Club House
Mayflower Arriving in Provincetown Harbor
Monument to Men of Boston
Old Man of the Mountain, Franconia, New Hampshire
Old South Church
Old Windmill, Nantucket Island
Pilgrim Exiles
Pilgrim Memorial Monument, Provincetown, Massachusetts
Public Library 1899
Return of the Mayflower
St. Anne's By the Sea, Kennebunkport, Maine
Washington Elm, Cambridge, Massachusetts
Wadsworth Longfellow House, Portland, Maine

WELLSVILLE CHINA COMPANY
Wellsville, Ohio
1879-

This company passed through several name changes but was still in business in the nineteen sixties.

Wellsville's 155th Anniversary, 1950, Chief Logan in center, six border scenes, black.

WEST CO. KILNS

Alaska, very similar to Vernon Kilns plates

C.E. WHEELOCK and COMPANY
Importer
South Bend, Indiana
later, Peoria, Illinois
1888-1971

The C.E. Wheelock Importing Company was a leader in the import business for many years. The Wheelock name will be found on the little china tumblers, pin trays, vases, and other trinkets sold in almost every town in the U.S. from the late 1880s almost to the beginning of World War II. This company also imported many blue plates but unfortunately did not have its mark impressed on every one. The most easily found blue plate is the eight inch type with five or six equal-sized views separated by floral scrolls. The majority will be marked only "England." Judging from the buildings and other features, most of these plates were made between 1900 and 1930. Beardmore, Adams, and others were the manufacturers.

Arch Rock, center scene, six border medallions, (Mackinack Island) scrolled border, blue, 10 inches

Arlington House, Hot Springs, Arkansas, blue

Athol, Massachusetts, souvenir of, blue-grey, 6 1/2 inches

Brownsville, Texas, blue

Canton, Illinois, five equal-size views

Cape Girardeau, Missouri, six views, blue, 7 1/2 inches

Catskill Mountains, New York, souvenir of, blue-grey, six views, 7 1/2 inches

Colorado State Capitol, blue, 10 inches

Crescent Hotel

Denver, Colorado, 8 inches

General George Meade, and Headquarters, Gettysburg, Pennsylvania, blue, 10 inches

General Robert E. Lee, blue, 10 inches

Gettysburg Commemorative, General Lee and Staff and Headquarters, blue, 10 inches

Gettysburg, views of, one view is of Meade's Headquarters, blue, 7 5/8 inches

Great Barrington, Massachusetts, 7 1/2 inches

Heart Islands, 1000 Islands

Hot Springs, Arkansas

Iowa State Capitol

Johnstown and Sacaudaga Park, pale blue, 7 3/4 inches

Lexington Park, Lexington, Massachusetts

Lincoln House, Springfield, Illinois, blue, 9 inches

Port Arthur, Texas, souvenir of, six views with narrow border, blue, 7 1/2 inches

St. Mary's Hospital, Rochester, Minnesota, blue, 8 inches

St. Louis World's Fair, blue, 1904

Thousand Islands, five border scenes, scalloped edge, deep blue, 9 inches (also made in 7 inch size)

U.S. Capitol, roses border, blue, 10 inches

Wichita, Kansas

F. WINKLE and COMPANY
Stoke
Staffordshire, England
1890-1931

This company made very attractive commemorative plates and seems to have specialized in western views. These western views are not nearly as numerous as eastern views, for obvious reasons. In addition to souvenir plates, the company made semi-porcelain dinner sets in bright blue and other colors. An interesting plate is one of the State Normal School at Cortland, New York. The border is from a dinner set called "Togo."

The company used the logo Colonial Pottery, Stoke, England, between 1890 and 1925.

City Hall, New York, blue, 1909, 9 1/2 inches

Cortland, New York, Normal School, floral border (Togo pattern border), bright blue, 9 3/4 inches

Denver, Colorado, City Park, border shows scenes of U.S. Mint, State Capitol, library and auditorium, separated by hepaticas, blue, 9 1/2 inches

Gettysburg, souvenir of, Meade's Headquarters

in center with insert of General Meade, floral border, bright blue, 9 inches

Harrisburg, State Capitol, "Togo" border, blue, 9 3/4 inches

Iowa State Capitol, floral border

Manchester in the Mountains, four border scenes, blue

Newark, New Jersey

Oakland, California, center is Taft and Kenoyer Building, four border scenes separated by sunflowers, blue, 9 1/2 inches

Richfield Springs, New York, "Togo" border

Saratoga Convention Hall, Rock Springs in center, soft blue, 10 inches

Seattle, Washington, center is Totem Pole surrounded by buildings, four border scenes, separated by sunflowers, blue, 9 1/2 inches

WOOD and SONS
Burslem, Staffordshire, England
1865-

This is another confusing mark as Godden lists twenty-seven different Wood potteries. The Wood and Sons which made commemorative plates also changed titles several times. The company seems to have been active in the commemorative field at the beginning of the twentieth century. Later, the emphasis seemed to be on Canadian views.

American Independence, 1776, scene of men in small boat, blue, 9 inches

Auburn, New York, center is post office, four border scenes, buildings in the Auburn vicinity including the state prison, bright blue, 9 inches

Brunswick, Evangeline, blue, 8 3/4 inches

First Church of Christ, Bradford, Massachusetts, blue, 10 inches

First M.E. Church of Boston

Hiawatha Portrait, blue

Landing of Carver, Bradford, Winslow, Standish, 10 inches

Primitive Methodist Centenary, multi-color, portraits of Bourne, Clowes, various chapels, 1807-1907, 9 3/4 and 10 inches

Pawtucket, Rhode Island, Congregational Church, 1829-1939, fruit, flowers, leaves border, 10 inches

Royal Canadian Mounties

Sailing Ships, blue, 10 inches, c. 1927, artist, A. M. Main, Jr., **America's Cup Defender Ranger**

S.S. Shenandoah, 1890-1910

St. Theresa's Church, West Roxbury, Massachusetts, 10 inches

Six Masted Schooner, Wyoming, 1919, fruit and flower border, blue

States Plate, fifteen states form chain around border, sunburst center, gold, blue, 9 inches (same design made by several other companies)

Transylvania University, blue

Union Line, deep blue, 9 1/8 inches

William and Mary College seal (in gold) in center, with first fifteen states in border, blue, 9 inches

WRIGHT, TYNDALE and VAN RODEN
Importers
Philadelphia, Pennsylvania
1818-1960

In the early years of this century the Wright, Tyndale, and Van Roden Company commissioned the Minton Potteries to make a series of about twenty views of Philadelphia and Pennsylvania. They are medium to dark blue, 9 1/2 inches. (See Minton section for more plates with the Wright, Tyndale and Van Roden backstamp.)

Bartram's House, soft, blurred blue

Betsy Ross House

Carpenter's Hall

Christ Church

Girard College

Landing of Lafayette, 1824

Penn's Treaty Tree, Philadelphia

Philadelphia Water Works

Stenton

Sunbury House on the Nishaminy

William Penn's Cottage, Letisha Court

others

YE OLD HISTORICAL POTTERY
YE OLDE HISTORICAL POTTERY

These backstamps are found on plates made by British Anchor Pottery and others. Quite often this is the only mark.

Sometimes there are registry numbers. A set or series was made before 1920. They are numbered from one to fifteen plus. They are all blue, and have four border scenes with small flowers between each of the oval border insets. See Rowland and Marsellus chapter for listing of these plates.

Battle of New Orleans
Faneuil Hall
Independence Hall
Landing of Hendrick Hudson
Landing of the Pilgrims
Niagara Falls
Patrick Henry
Washington Crossing the Delaware

The items listed below were described in the ads as being marked England or Staffordshire. They could be anything from pre-Jones, McDuffee and Stratton to ENCO.

Atlantic City, narrow leaf border, blue, 9 3/4 inches
Battle Creek, Michigan, blue, 10 inches
Battle Monument, Baltimore, pink, 9 inches
Fiftieth Anniversary, Battle of Gettysburg, 1863-1913, scenes of Pennsylvania State Memorial, Lee's and Meade's Headquarters, portraits of Lee and Meade and Confederate flags
Battle of New Orleans, 1907, blue, 9 inches
Battlefield Cartoon, World War I, signed Bruce Bainsfeather, with poem, made 1917 by girls when boys were in trenches fighting for liberty and civilization, 7 1/2 inches
Biddeford, Maine
Boston, Massachusetts, views of, deep blue, 9 inches
Boulder Dam, 10 inches
Chautauqua, New York, six scenes, blue
Coolidge Home, deep blue
Commemorating McDonough's Victory, blue, 10 inches
Concord, Massachusetts, souvenir of, Minute Man Statue, six border scenes, blue, 7 1/8 inches
Daytona, Florida
Detroit, Michigan, blue, 9 inches
Fredericksburg, Kenmore, pink, 7 3/4 inches

Fulham Church, blue
Gloucester, Massachusetts, tile, Oldest Universalist Church in America, brown, 6 1/4 inches
Hartford, historic, views of
Holyoke, Massachusetts, Oldest Church
Home of Thomas Jefferson, at Monticello, lavender, 10 1/2 inches
Horseshoe Curve, Pennsylvania, scalloped edge, Wm. Gable and Co. **Dept. Store, Altoona, Pennsylvania**, deep blue
Hudson-Fulton Tercentenary, 1909, blue, 7 1/2 inches
Hudson-Fulton 1909, Hotel Astor, blue, 8 inches
Hudson-Fulton, 1909, Statue of Liberty, blue
Jacksonville, Florida, souvenir of, Florida scenes in border, deep blue, 10 inches
Lincoln Memorial, 10 inches
Los Angeles, California, views of, dark blue
Massachusetts State Capitol, blue
Milwaukee
Minneapolis, post in center, blue and green, 10 inches
Minnehaha Falls, Minnesota, 1902, blue, 7 1/2 inches
Monticello, made for Charlottesville Hardware Co., Virginia, mulberry
Mohawk Trail, blue, 7 1/2 inches
Nantucket, blue, 10 inches
National Monument to Forefathers, Plymouth, Massachusetts, poem on back, blue, 9 3/4 inches
Natural Bridge, Virginia, blue, 10 inches
Newbergh, New York, Washington's Headquarters, 1763-1863, blue, 7 inches
New Bedford, Massachusetts, blue, 9 inches
New Haven, Connecticut, narrow leaf border, blue, 9 1/4 inches
Niagara Falls, blue, 10 inches, 9 inches
Norristown, 100th Anniversary, 1912
Norwich, Connecticut, 1909, blue, 8 inches
Old Historic Salem, North Carolina, lavender
Old Point Comfort, Virginia, cup and saucer, blue
Old Scituate Light, Scituate, Massachusetts, blue, 7 3/4 inches
Panama-California Exposition, San Diego, scalloped edge, shows state normal school, U.S. Grant Hotel, public library, San Diego Mission, blue, 8 3/4 inches
Patrick Henry Addressing the Virginia Assembly, reg. no.563729, blue
Philadelphia City Hall
Pilgrim Memorial Monument, blue, 9 inches
Pittsburgh, Pennsylvania, blue
Plymouth Rock, 1906, rock in center, scenes in border
Plymouth, souvenir of, seven views, 1907, blue
Portland, Maine, City Hall, etc., blue
Portland, Oregon, Centennial, 1905, blue
Provincetown, Pilgrim Monument

Retreat of the British at Concord, April 19, 1775, deep blue, 10 inches
Rhode Island, state of, deep blue
Roosevelt, 10 inches
Ride of Paul Revere, blue, 10 inches
St. John, New Brunswick, views of, blue, 10 inches
San Jose, California, deep blue
Springfield, Massachusetts, blue, 9 inches
Syracuse, historical views of
Table Rock, Niagara, blue, 10 inches
Tennessee, commemorative of, blue, 10 inches
Twin Lights, Chatham, Cape Cod, blue, 9 inches
Union Line, blue, 10 inches
Washington Crossing the Delaware, blue, 9 3/4 inches
Washington, D.C., border is cherry leaves, six pictures of historic sites, blue, 9 1/4 inches
Washington State, blue, 9 inches
West Point, blue, 10 inches
Whirlpool Rapids, 10 inches
Winona, Minnesota, blue, 10 inches
Woonsocket, Rhode Island, blue, 9 inches
Zanesville, Ohio, souvenir of, Old Y Bridge, Monumental Building, Courthouse, Masonic Lodge, and New Y Bridge

---

This final list is of items where no indication of age or origin was given in the ads.

Abe Lincoln, picture of Lincoln at top, copy of letter to Mrs. Bixby and log cabin at bottom, octagonal, blue, 8 inches
Abraham Lincoln portrait, border shows Iowa state capitol, Fort Des Moines, officers, soldiers' and sailors' monument, Sixth Avenue Bridge, Polk County courthouse, blue
Admiral Nimitz, Allied Nations Commanders series, flag and eagle border, colorful, 10 3/4 inches
Admiral Perry, Lake Erie
Albany, state capitol, souvenir of
Allen Thurman picture (ran with Cleveland for vice-president), 8 inches
Allentown, Pennsylvania, blue, 7 3/4 inches
Allied Nations, Commemorative, multi-colored border, shows Allied flags, General MacArthur, Admiral King, and probably others, 11 inches
American flag in center and Old Glory, red, white and blue stripes on edge, 10 inches
American Pottery, New York World's Fair, 1939, exhibition of capital and labor

Ashland, Ohio
Bar Harbor, Maine, center shows Bar Harbor, border is Balance Rock, etc., blue, 9 inches
Battery and Sea Wall, Charleston, South Carolina, 7 inches
Battleship Maine, deep blue, dish
Benjamin Franklin, 1706-1906, deep blue
Beverly, Massachusetts, summer home of President Taft, United Shoe Machinery Company, etc., blue, 8 inches
Brandon, Manitoba, blue, 7 inches
Bridgewater, Massachusetts, bicentennial, blue
Bryant and Longfellow, pitcher, 7 inches
Brooklyn Bridge, black, 9 inches
Boulder, the, Lexington, Massachusetts, line of the Minute Men, April 19, 1775, "stand your ground, etc.," 8 1/4 inches
Burlington, views of
Callao School Building, Missouri, 7 inches
Cape Cod, blue, 7 1/2 inches
Capital and Labor, 1939, blue, 7 inches
Capitol Island, Maine, old sailing ships, etc., pink, 8 1/2 inches
Carnegie Free Library, Ogden, Utah, 7 1/2 inches
Catskill Mountains, Rip Van Winkle in center, blue, 9 inches
Cedarville, Kansas, Mercantile Building, 10 inches
Charles A. Lindbergh, flight and events to then, chrome yellow, 10 inches
Chevy Chase, blue, 9 and 7 inches
Cheyenne, Wyoming, blue, 8 inches
Chief Wolf Robe, colors, 11 1/2 inches
Churchill and Roosevelt, small bowl
Cleveland, souvenir of, five scenes, small inset of James Garfield
Cliff Rock and Seal Rock, San Francisco, blue
Cocksackie, New York, souvenir of, bearded Rip Van Winkle
Colorado Springs, views of, 9 inches
Compliments of John Hedin Furniture, Cambridge, Massachusetts, advertising plate, flow blue, raised rim, 10 inches
Confederate Monument, Dallas Texas, made for Doolittle, Simpson, of Dallas, deep blue
Congregational Church, Oxford, Maine, with history, 10 inches
Congressional Library, 1900, brown, 9 inches; same-Capitol, White House, Washington Monument
Connecticut Tercentennial, courthouse scenes, border is grape design with names of cities
Courthouse, Allentown, Pennsylvania, blue
Courthouse, Baltimore, Maryland, deep blue, 8 1/2 inches
Courthouse, Syracuse, New York, blue, 10 inches
Crawford Cooking Ranges, platter, blue, 8 1/2 by 11 inches

Daniel Webster

Dartmouth College, Hanover, New Hampshire, Webster Hall, Rollins Chapel, etc., blue, 6 inches

Davey Crockett Ceramic jug, for 1936 Texas Centennial

Dayton, Ohio, centennial, jumbo cup and saucer, 1896

Denver, souvenir of, blue, 7 3/4 inches

Detroit, souvenir of, cake salver, Old City Hall, dedicated in 1871, brown

Doe-Wah-Jack, full figure framed by wreath of oak leaves, advertising for Round Oak Stoves, green, 9 inches

Don't Give Up the Ship, blue

Douglas Aircraft Company, California, first twenty years, 1920-1940, pictures four bombers, blue, 10 inches

Dueling Tree, New Orleans, mulberry

Duxbury, Massachusetts, Myles Standish monument, John Alden House, Powder Point Hall, etc., blue, 7 3/4 inches

Elsie the Cow, by Borden Company

Evangeline, "Down the long street she passed," blue, 10 inches

Famous Lawrence Mansion, blue, 8 1/2 inches

Faneuil Hall, Boston, scalloped border, green, 10 1/2 inches

Faneuil Hall from the Harbor, blue

First Baptist Church at Norfolk, Virginia

First Fort Dearborn, 9 inches

Flatiron Building, New York City

Flint, Michigan, views of

Founders Day Banquet, souvenir of, November 17, 1910, 125th anniversary of General Society of Mechanics and Tradesmen of the **City of New York**, scalloped edge, deep blue, 10 inches

Francis Willard commemorative, centenary 1839-1939, W.C.T.U. founder, blue, 10 inches

Franklin Pierce portrait, 1852-1857, center is black, flags are brown on cream, 8 1/2 inches

Franklin Roosevelt, wide gold border, 10 3/4 inches

F.D. Roosevelt, blue with gold border

Friends Meeting House, Salem, New Jersey, embossed border, black

Fredericksburg, historical, border scenes of old buildings, dark blue, 10 inches

Garfield, black transfer on ironstone, 7 3/4 inches

General MacArthur, made during his command of Far East Forces, blue, 10 1/2 inches

General Meade's Headquarters, blue, 10 inches

George Washington bust after Gilbert Stuart, impressed scalloped rim, made for Friends Tavern, oldest within U.S. in continued use, sepia, 9 inches

George Washington's Initiation as Free Mason, blue, 9 inches

Gettysburg, souvenir of, General Meade's Headquarters in center, border portraits of generals, blue, 10 inches

Gloucester, Massachusetts, scenes of fishing schooners, thatchers, lights, Glocester salt, etc., blue, 7 1/2 inches

Golden Gate Exposition, 1939, official souvenir of, china, 10 inches

Graf Zeppelin plate

Grant's Causeway North, 8 inches

Great Barrington, Massachusetts, souvenir of, six views, blue, 7 1/2 inches

Green Bay, Wisconsin, views of

Green Falls, Lewiston, Maine, 7 1/2 inches

Gray Gables, Buzzard's Bay, Massachusetts, 6 1/2 inches

Grey Hound bus, advertising, blue

Grover Cleveland for President, Adlai Stevenson for V.P., 1892

Grover Cleveland and Allen Thurman, heads, ironstone, pitcher

Hampton Beach, New Hampshire, 6 1/2 inches

Harper's Ferry, Virginia, blue, 7 3/4 inches

Harrisburg, Pennsylvania, views of, blue, 9 inches

Hartford, Vermont, souvenir of, Gibson Girl with man in rowboat, 6 1/4 inches

Harvard College Gateway, scalloped edge, green, 9 1/2 inches

Haverhill, Mass., Whittier's Birthplace, city hall, post office, etc., blue, 10 inches

Highland Light, Cape Cod, Massachusetts, blue, 8 inches

Historic New Jersey, 10 1/2 inches

Historic Salem, North Carolina (imported by Arden Farm Store), mulberry, 10 inches

Historic Trenton, New Jersey, six scenes, Washington Crossing the Delaware, blue

Hoboken, New Jersey, blue, 7 inches

Home of Lincoln, squatty pitcher, embossed mulberries

Home of President Taft, Beverly, Massachusetts, 7 1/4 inches

Homes of the Presidents, White House rooms, 7 1/2 inches

Hood's Texas Brigade Assn., 1967 and 1968 (two plates)

House of the Seven Gables, Story Book Plates, blue, 7 3/4 inches

Indiana Territory Sesquicentennial, Capitol Building center, 1950, deep blue, 10 inches

Indianapolis, Indiana, black, 10 inches

Indianapolis, signed A. Sunn, 1908, 9 inches

Iola's Big Gun, Iola, Kansas, 8 inches

Iowa Soldier's Home, Marshall, Iowa, 7 3/4 inches

J. Horne, Pittsburgh, blue, 10 inches

Jacksonville, Florida, deep blue, 10 inches and 7 3/4 inches

58

James Garfield, ironstone pitcher, eagle spout and handle, portrait in relief on front and back, 8 1/2 inches

Jamestown, blue

John Alden and Priscilla, Mayflower tea set, black with blue trim transfer, sugar, creamer, tea pot, cake plate, 2 tea plates, 2 cups and saucers

John Alden and Priscilla, green, 9 1/2 inches

John Dewey portrait, cobalt trim

Kahler, the, Rochester, Minnesota, 8 1/2 inches

Kenmore, home of only sister of George Washington, tile, blue

Keokuk, Iowa

King's Chapel, Bowdoin College, Maine, blue, 10 inches

Kingston, New York, blue, 7 3/4 inches

Lackawanna R.A.C. No. 185, 1856-1905, Scranton, Pennsylvania, anniversary plate

La Crosse, Wisconsin, town scenes, blue, 9 inches

Le Creole Academy and Dalles College, Dalles, Oregon, butterpat

Lakewood, New Jersey, large center scene, border scenes, blue, 10 inches

Lake Champlain, New York, souvenir of, steamer Vermont, Fort Ticonderoga, ruins, etc., blue, 7 5/8 inches

Landing of Lafayette, blue, 9 inches

L.C. Alen Mercantile Company, Cedarvale, Kansas, coupe shape, blue, 7 1/2 inches

Libby Prison in Wartime, Confederate flags, etc.

Lincoln, Gettysburg, Pennsylvania, monument, speech on back

Lincoln pitcher, blue, 15 inches tall

Los Angeles, views of, six scenes, 7 3/4 inches

Los Angeles Courthouse, border scenes, four missions, deep blue, 9 inches

Louisiana Purchase 1803-1904, Jefferson in center with scenes in border, blue, 10 1/2 inches

Lusitania, soups, black, 9 inches

MacArthur commemorative, blue, 10 1/2 inches

Map of Panama Canal, green border of presidents' heads, flags, etc., same in dark blue with gold border, Old Glory, 1915, 8 1/2 inches

Mark Twain's Birthplace, Florida, Missouri, blue, 6 inches

Martha Washington states plate, deep blue, 9 inches

McKinley

Methodist Church, South Orange, New Jersey, black with cream border

Milwaukee, Wisconsin, city hall, etc., blue

Minneapolis, scenic border, blue

Minnehaha Falls, Minneapolis, blue, 1903, 7 1/2 inches

Minnesota, scenic border, blue

Missouri-Pacific Line, multi-colored border shows flowers of 11 states, center is speeding locomotive, (railroad china?), 10 1/2 inches

Missouri scenes, 9 inches

Mobile, Alabama, center, six border scenes

Mohawk Trail, souvenir of, blue, 7 1/2 inches

Monticello, red center, blue stippled border, gold edge, 11 inches

Montreal, blue, 6 3/4 inches

Mormon Temples

Montgomery Ward best china of 1870s; **Spirit of '76, Crossing the Delaware**, (square plates), 8 1/2 inches, purple, pink; platter, purple, 9 by 12 inches; tea pot finial is head of Puritan, pink

Monticello, Home of Jefferson, Jefferson's head in medallion at top, other scenes, scrolled border, 1939, blue, 10 1/2 inches

Mound City, Illinois centennial, 1854-1954, blue

Mt. Ranier from Seattle, 7 inches

Mt. Vernon, colors, 8 inches

Mugs, marked Collector, colors, portraits of **Paul Revere, Betsy Ross, Anthony Wayne, John Paul Jones**

Mysterious Stone Tower, Newport, Rhode Island, 8 1/2 inches

Nag's Head, North Carolina

Nahank River, New York

Nantucket, scenic border, blue

Nantucket, grey-blue, 7 3/4 inches

Nantucket, Massachusetts, pitcher, shows oldest house in Nantucket, blue, 7 inches

National Monument to our Forefathers, Massachusetts, deep blue, fruit and flower border, verse on back, 9 3/4 inches

New Capitol, the, Richmond, Virginia, blue, 7 1/2 inches

New London, views of, blue

Newport, views of, blue

New York, official souvenir, center scene is George Washington, blue

New York University, 1932, blue

Niagara Falls, scenic border, blue, 7 inches

Niagara Falls, floral border, blue, 10 1/2 inches

North Carolina, Tar Heel State, 5 views, 10 inches

Ohio Sesquicentennial, Matthews House, Lake County, etc.

Old Bay Line, 1940, pictorial map of Virginia and Maryland, border is five steamers used between Baltimore and Norfolk; Baltimore **Steam Packet**, the oldest steamboat company in the U.S., 10 1/2 inches

Old Burnham Tavern, Machias, Maine, square, 5 inches

Old Glory, center is map of Panama Canal, dates begun and finished, border has oval portraits of all presidents, top shows American flag and shield, letters "Old Glory" compliments of Ludwig Furniture Co., Perth Amboy, New Jersey

Old Meeting House, Townsend, Massachusetts, 10 inches

Old Mill, Clinton Academy, blue, 10 1/2 inches

Old Oak Burial Ground, Salem, New Jersey, black with cream embossed border

Old Tabernacle, Newark, New Jersey, red and white

Old Town Hall, Marblehead, Massachusetts, border scenes, blue, 8 inches

Oldest Universalist Church in America, Gloucester, Massachusetts, tile, round, brown, 6 1/2 inches

Opening of the St. Lawrence Seaway, Canada and U.S., 1959

Oregon, state, Lewis and Clark, Indians, 10 other scenes,brown, 1900, 11 inches

Ottawa, Illinois, views of, Masonic Temple, etc., blue, 9 inches

Our Choice, 1908, sepia, William Howard Taft

Owl's Head, Maine, deep blue

Pacific Fleet, the

Pentecostal Temple Church, Memphis, Tennessee, red

Perry, Maine, sesquicentennial, 1818-1968, history on back, blue, 11 inches

Perry Memorial, blue

Philadelphia, China Hall, 1876

Pittsburgh Exposition, green, old block house, backstamped, Kaufman's the Big Store, etc., blue, 8 inches

Plymouth Rock, Ye Old Historical Pottery, lavender, 10 inches

Poughkeepsie Bridge, Height 212 feet, Poughkeepsie, New York, blue, 9 inches

President Buchanan's Home, blue

Presidential Mansion, impressed picture, majolica, French?, bright green, 9 inches

Presidents, 1953, blue

Presidents' Wives, Mrs. Washington, Mrs. Lincoln, Mrs. T. Roosevelt

Prospect Point, American and Horseshoe Falls, blue, 7 3/4 inches

Providence, Rhode Island, souvenir of, shows Union Depot, Arcade, etc., blue, 6 3/4 inches

Providence, Rhode Island, views of, State House, etc., blue

Quebec, souvenir of, blue, 7 3/4 inches

Queen Elizabeth and Philip, visit of 1957

Railroad China, made for "The Traveler" Milwaukee Road, 1920s, pink geese, fir trees, white background

Red Hook, New York, ironstone, floral and scenic border

Remember Pearl Harbor, 10 1/2 inches

Remember the Maine, eagle and U.S. shield, colorful red, white and blue, 8 1/2 inches

Republican Centennial, porcelain, profiles of Lincoln and Eisenhower, 10 inches

Retreat of British from Concord, blue

Rockland, Maine, souvenir of, breakwater, light, Owl's Head, etc., blue, 7 1/2 inches

St. Augustine, coat of arms, border is green, gold, white, flowers, 8 inches

St. Louis World's Fair, 1904, jumbo cup and saucer, Palace of Arts, Administration Building, Fisheries Building, saucer is 8 1/2 inches

St. Louis World's Fair, 1904, Palace of Textiles, green on ivory, 10 inches

St. Petersburg, Florida, blue, 8 inches

St. Vincent's Rock, blue, 10 inches

Salt Lake City, souvenir of, five scenes, clusters of fruit between scenes, blue, 9 inches

Salt Lake City, tumbler, Brigham Young's Monument, Temple Block, Eagle Gate. etc., blue, 3 3/8 inches tall

Salem Reformed Church, Allentown, Pennsylvania, 8 3/4 inches

Savannah, seven scenes, mulberry, 10 1/2 inches

Seattle, Washington, rolled rim, six border scenes, blue, 10 inches

Sharon Springs, New York

Sippewisset, Indian, colorful, border is Indian symbols, blue and earth, 10 inches

Sitting Bull, Buffalo Bill, Annie Oakley, etc., 7 inches

S.S. Christopher Columbus, Chicago, Milwaukee Route, colorful, gold border, 8 inches

South Dakota, "Under God the People Rule," bright colors, scene of man plowing, 10 inches

Spanish War Commemorative, U.S.S. Texas

Spokane, Washington

Spokane Falls

Springfield, Illinois, six scenes, blue, 9 inches

State House, Augusta, Maine, 7 inches

Standish House, Duxbury, Connecticut, 1666, 10 inches

Statue of Liberty, blue, 10 inches

Statue of Liberty, blue, rolled edge, 10 inches

Stillwater, Minnesota, souvenir of, Betsy Ross sewing flag while officers watch, 7 1/2 inches

Swift County Courthouse, Benson, Minnesota, 6 1/2 inches

Teddy Roosevelt, full bust, border, red and blue bands

Territory of Hawaii, Alaska-Yukon-Pacific Exposition, Seattle, 1909, Territory of Hawaii, U.S.A., center is phoenix bird,seal, etc., 9 inches

Texas Bicentennial, designed by Texas etcher, Willie Rowe, porcelain, blue

Texas Under Six Flags, 1936, centennial exposition, porcelain, shows flags, 8 1/2 inches

Tidewater, Virginia, Captain John Smith, center, Williamsburg, Norfolk, Jamestown, deep blue, 10 inches (1906)

Trinity College, six memorial plates, black, 8 inches

Thirteen states, creamer, blue, 5 inches

Toronto

Town Muldoon, in the commonwealth of Massachusetts, 10 1/4 inches

Twelfth Regiment Leads War for the Union, china, light blue, with gold edge, May 2, 1899, 9 inches, covered with information, back and front, center picture is Crossing the Bridge into Virginia

Three Brides, Historic Nantucket Houses, handpainted, embossed border

Trenton, New Jersey, 250th anniversary, 1929, Old Barracks

University of Washington, light blue, 10 inches

United States Congressional Library, 7 1/2 inches

United States Congressional Library, purple, 7 inches

U.S. Maine, platter, deep blue

United States Seal, colorful border, cup and saucer, Cuban and American flags

Utah, Pioneer Jubilee, cup, western scene, obverse seal of state and bison

Utah, state, Mormon scenes, 1857-1896, 9 inches, 10 inches, shows temple, White Throne, Great Seal of Utah

Valley Forge, 1910, blue

Vassar College, blue, 9 inches

Virgin Islands, 7 inches

Washington Birthplace, Bicentenary, flow blue

Washington and Lafayette at Mt. Vernon, blue, 10 1/2 inches (roses border)

Washington and Lafayette at Mt. Vernon, memorial, 1732-1932, blue, 10 1/2 inches

Wells Cathedral, Newark, red

Wharton House

White House, National Historic Plate, 9 inches

White House plate and platter with cut corners, after 1912

White House in color, presidents up to Wilson around border, plate 9 1/8 inches

White Mountains, views of, rolled edge, blue

Wilkes Barre, Pennsylvania, views of, five scenes, blue, 9 inches

Whittier House, Danvers, scalloped border, green, 10 1/2 inches

Will Rogers, shows memorials dedicated to him, mulberry, 10 inches

William Harrison, Fort Meigs, deep blue, 8 inches

William Jennings Bryan, scalloped border, green lustre, 9 inches

William Penn, Bucks County, Bicentennial, cup and saucer, 1882

William Taft portrait, lustre rim

Winnipeg, Manitoba

Winona, Dice's Head, octagonal, blue, 5 inches

"Wolfe Robe," a Cheyenne Chief, rust on yellow, 9 1/4 inches

Woodrow Wilson, hexagonal tile, white bust on pale blue

Wood's Hotel, Ripon, Wisconsin, 1878, Nov. 28 reg. date, pitcher, brown, 3 1/2 inches picture of hotel with floral decor

Woodstock, Vermont, Inn, 6 1/2 inches

Worcester, Massachusetts scenes

World War Memorial, Augusta, Maine, deep blue, 9 1/2 inches

World Columbian Exposition, Agricultural Building, A.B.C.plate, embossed alphabet, blue, 7 5/8 inches

World's Fair Administration Building, Chicago, 1933, square, 5 inches

World's Fair, New York, 1939, Unisphere in center, decorated by Charles Murphy, 150th anniversary of George Washington's Inauguration, 10 inches

World's Fair, St. Louis, 1904, Palace of Electricity, deep blue, 10 1/2 inches

World's Fair, 1893, Santa Maria, 7 inches

Zoar Hotel, Zoar, Ohio, 1933, four border scenes, picture of hotel in center, blue on cream, 10 inches

ORIENTAL IMPORTS

Within the past fifteen years, many historic sites and tourist attractions have turned to Japan for commemoratives. Many of them are copies of popular designs such as the five-view and the coupe shape. The copies are generally light in color. Also many are porcelain, not earthenware. The only identification is a small paper sticker. The earthenware copies are often rather heavy with a clunky feeling. They too have only a paper sticker. A beginning collector would be well advised to buy only clearly marked items. There are many "newer" plates from England, made by companies such as Adams. These are always backstamped with the country of origin and the maker's mark. Firms such as Jonroth and Enco have never tried to deceive anyone into thinking that their wares are old. Because they are marked, they can be considered "collectible" or the antiques of the future.

SOUVENIR PLATE PATTERNS

Prices listed are for pieces in "mint" condition. Since souvenir plates were meant for decoration rather than for daily use, there should be no allowance for wear from usage. Prices were determined from shops, malls, shows, auctions, and antique and collector publications in the Midwest. Prices will be about 10 to 15 percent higher on either coast.

Subject matter and intensity of color also affect price. For example, souvenirs from the 1904 St. Louis World's Fair are avidly sought after in the St. Louis area and the prices reflect that demand. Also, scarcity, including limited edition pieces such as anniversary and special occasion pieces (made only once), affects prices.

Adams

1. Adena, Home of Thomas Worthington, designed and imported for the Ohio Historical Society (after 1953), not old but collectible because of subject matter and design. $12.

2. Barbara Fritchie's Home, Frederick, Maryland, prototype of hundreds of views imported by Jonroth between the early 1930s and 1965. $6.

3. Bellingrath Gardens, cup and saucer, about 1964. $12.

4. Bermuda, Government House, could have been part of a set or series, very early Adams, about 1909. $50.

5. Same view with a black center (Wedgwood made a similar example about 1900—see Wedgwood section for picture). $55.

6. Bunker Hill Monument about 1905, could be unmarked French, Mitchell, Woodbury import; although not popular with collectors, these odd colors (such as green or pink) are very uncommon. $25.

7. Bunker Hill Monument in the more common blue, about 1905. $35.

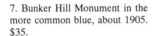

8. Cannon Memorial Chapel, University of Richmond, probably one of a series of six or twelve plates from about 1955. $10.

9. The Capitol, Adams Souvenir Series, 1929, coupe shape; the narrow floral border is a common Jonroth feature. $25.

10. Backstamp and impressed date of the Adams Souvenir Series used between circa 1920 and 1935.

11. Citrus Tower, Clermont, Florida, same border as The Capitol plate but much later, about 1965. $10.

12. Cliff House and Seal Rocks, innovative design, called vignette style. $20.

13. Information on back of Cliff House plate indicating date of manufacture—1958.

14. Fall River Pass Store, Rocky Mountain National Park, (many of these late examples might someday be very collectible as they were made in limited quantities for small local businesses). $5.

15. Florida state plate, common, typical late Jonroth. $8.

16. Flowing Well (Titusville, Pennsylvania?), early, unmarked example, could be a French, Mitchell, Woodbury import which would date it between 1901 and 1905. $45.

17. Franciscan Monastery, Washington, D.C., very late (not Jonroth), line drawing rather than a photograph, late 1970s. $3.

18. Franconia Notch, Old Man of the Mountain, tile, Adams Souvenir series, copy of style originated by Wedgwood, about 1930. $20.

19. George Washington Masonic National Memorial plate, Alexandria, Virginia, late example worth collecting because of limited time and number made. $15.

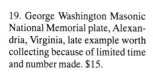

20. Grand Hotel, Mackinac Island, Michigan, copy of an earlier style featuring border scenes. $20.

21. Home of Daniel Webster, partial tea set, about 1925, saucer and plate. $15. each.

22. House of the Seven Gables, Adams Souvenir Series, about 1930, pitchers like this one were popular for many years and were made in a variety of sizes. $35.

71

23. Lincoln's Birthplace (creative photography?), the actual cabin is housed in a large marble building. $7.

24. Lincoln's New Salem, cup and saucer, saucer is "generic," could be used with any view cup, 1970s. $10.

25. Longfellow's Wayside Inn, butter pat size, very late, line drawing rather than a photo. $3.

26. Lincoln's New Salem, large size pitcher, style first imported in the 1960s. $20.

27. Mackinack Island, about 1920, the floral border almost overpowers the center scenes. $40.

28. Mason City, Illinois Centennial, 1957, unusual calendar border, could have been designed by Ellen Dearborn who owned the White Barn Antique Shop for which the plate was made. $20.

29. Mayflower, gadroon border, usually associated with Copeland. $35.

30. Back of Mayflower plate with quote from Mourt's Relation or Journal describing the sighting of land.

31. My Old Kentucky Home, portrait of Stephen Collins Foster on the reverse; the smallest size cup (2 1/2 inches) and saucer made. $15.

32. Moose Jaw, Saskatchewan, Canada, ashtray, unusual color overlay, about 1940. $15.

33. Old Church Tower, Jamestown, Virginia, 1957.
$15.

34. Old Oaken Bucket, Scituate, Maine, c. 1904,
could be a French, Mitchell, Woodbury import. $40.

35. Patriotic Ware, c. 1925 or a little earlier, 12 inch chop plate with holes in rim for hanging, part of a dinner set. $40.

36. Patriotic Ware, souvenir, Toledo, Ohio. $20.

37. Patriotic Ware, souvenir, St. Augustine, Florida, with heraldic emblem. $25.

38. E. Pluribus Unum, lunch plate to dinner set. $15.

39. Patriotic Ware, small tea pot, part of a tea set? $35.

40. Patriotic Ware, tankard shaped creamer with Arms of New York. $25.

41. Patriotic Ware, Dominion of Canada plate. $15.

42. Pilgrim Memorial Monument, tile, later than first example shown, possibly 1950s. $15.

43. Plymouth Rock, identical to rolled edge plates first imported by Rowland and Marsellus, 1920s. $45.

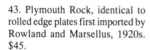

44. Royal Gorge, Colorado, view on one side only, 2 3/4 inches, smallest size made, 1950s. $10.

45. St. Louis World's Fair, unusual color, part of a
set, Palace of Electricity, same border as French,
Mitchell, Woodbury imports. $50.

46. St. Louis World's Fair, Palace
of Liberal Arts. $70.

47. St. Louis World's Fair, Palace of Machinery. $70.

48. State House, Boston, made for Jordan Marsh, department store backstamps will be found on plates made between 1900 and about 1940. $25.

49. Temple Square, Salt Lake City, 4 inch pitcher, 1950. $20.

50. Turkey Run State Park, The Inn, backstamp does not give location of the park which is in Indiana. $12.

51. U.S. Capitol, imported by Bowman (pre-1930). $40.

52. U.S. Capitol, same center scene as previous example. $40.

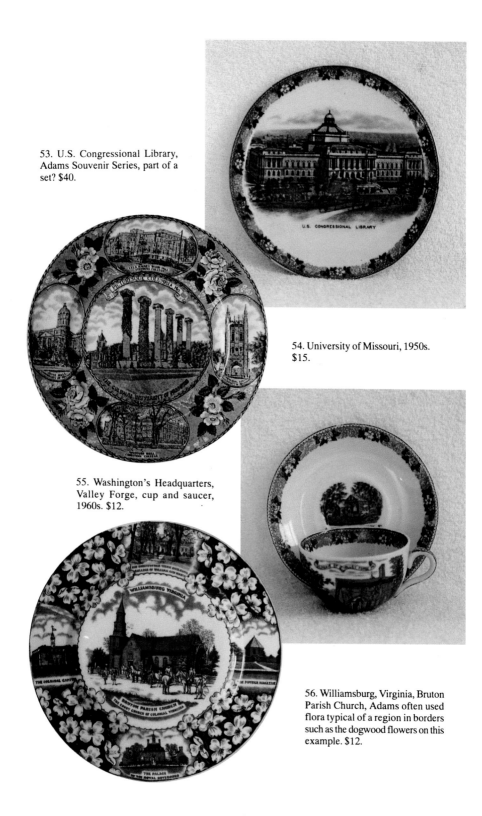

53. U.S. Congressional Library, Adams Souvenir Series, part of a set? $40.

54. University of Missouri, 1950s. $15.

55. Washington's Headquarters, Valley Forge, cup and saucer, 1960s. $12.

56. Williamsburg, Virginia, Bruton Parish Church, Adams often used flora typical of a region in borders such as the dogwood flowers on this example. $12.

57. Battle of Lake Erie, rare, blue with color applied. $95.

58. Federal Hall, color overlay with lustre. $100.

59. Independence Hall, rare, color overlay. $100.

60. Jacksonville, Florida, identical to Rowland and Marsellus examples. $70.

61. Miami, Florida. $65.

62. St. Augustine, Florida. $60.

63. Washington Crossing the Delaware. $70.

64. Whirlpool Rapids, Niagara Falls, green with color overlay. $90.

65. Backstamp, Bawo and Dotter.

It may seem redundant to show so many similar views, but as the popularity of these plates increases, reproductions will appear as they did with items such as Depression glass, historic flow blue, and even Fiesta ware. Collectors need to know what was made originally; this is best done by study and by handling pieces that are known to be old.

66. American College Plate with motto "The Pen is Mightier than the Sword." $40.

67. Boston, 6 views, a prototype of literally hundreds of views made for almost every city in the United States (Canada too). Many Japanese imports are copying this style. The imports are never marked. Also, they are light blue semi-porcelain, not earthenware. $15.

69. Denver, views of, slate blue. $25.

68. Coats of Arms of the United States of America, also made in blue. $25.

70. Indianapolis, Indiana, State House, stylized tulip border appears to have been a trademark of Beardmore. $30.

71. Kenton, Ohio, coupe shape plates like this seem to be common, and they are—in the aggregate, but there probably were never more than a few hundred made of any one view. $20.

72. Lincoln High School, Seattle, Washington, a good example of a limited appeal view. $15.

73. Minnehaha Falls, Minneapolis, Minnesota, type sold at souvenir stands in parks and at scenic attractions. $20.

74. Miles Standish House, borderless style, seems to have been a Beardmore trait. $15.

National Emblem plates, not part of a World War I Allies series, Austria-Hungary is included and also Beardmore was out of business by 1913.

75. Austria-Hungary emblem. $15.

76. France. $15.

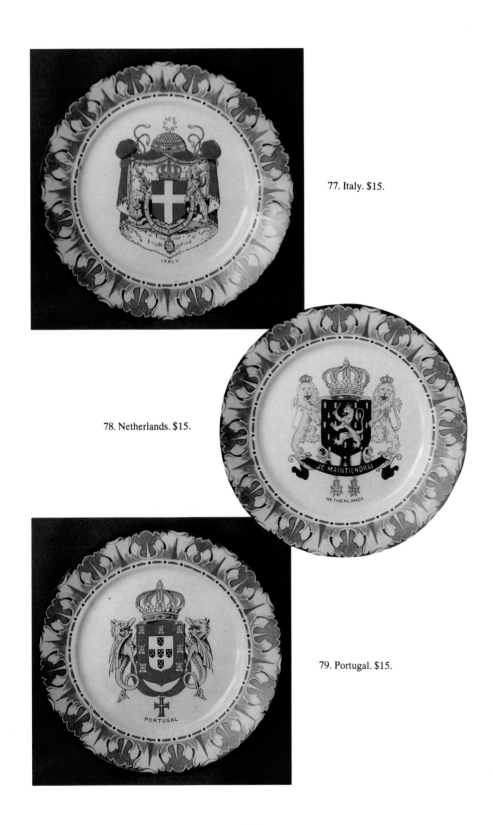

77. Italy. $15.

78. Netherlands. $15.

79. Portugal. $15.

80. Spain. $15.

81. Sweden. $15.

82. United States of America. $20.

83. Backstamp—there could have been more in this series, it would be logical to assume that all major European countries would have been included.

90

Bedford

84. Natural Bridge of Virginia, tile, copied from Adams or Wedgwood? $10.

85. Mt. LeConte, Great Smokey Mountains National Park. $12.

86. Salt Lake City cup and saucer, almost identical to examples made by Adams for Jonroth (the saucer is more interesting than the cup—it has the seal of Utah in the center). $20.

Bennett

87. Washington, D.C., could have been made for a specific event, round tents with Washington Monument in background. $30.

Bosselman

88. Landing of Henry Hudson, marked Boffleman, misprint for Bosselman? Also marked Rowland and Marsellus. $65.

89. Plymouth, Massachusetts, clear bright blue typical of Bosselman imports. $60.

90. Backstamp showing Bosselman misprint.

91. Capitol, Washington, D.C., appears to be Rowland and Marsellus, but backstamped Bowman. $50.

92. Penn's Treaty with the Indians. $55.

93. Sometimes the backstamps are as interesting as the view, this one reads "William Penn's Treaty with the Indians, 1683. It was the only treaty never sworn to and the only one never broken."

94. United States Capitol, atypical border, see Doulton section for more common Bowman border style. $40.

95. Battle of Bunker Hill, late example—has smooth rather than rippled border. $40.

96. Boston Massacre, another late example. $40.

97. Faneuil Hall from the Harbor. $50.

98. Mammoth Cave, view of underground restaurant, probably late 1940. $40.

99. Natural Bridge saucer, 1960s. $20.

100. Perry's Victory on Lake Erie, della robbia border, before 1950. $40.

101. Put-in-Bay, Ohio, early example, before 1920. $25.

102. Washington Crossing the Delaware, identical to Rowland and Marsellus imports. $55.

103. Independence Hall. $40.

104. Home of Emma Willard, part of a tea set for the Women's Christian Temperance Union? $50.

97

105. United States Capitol. $40.

106. The White House. $40.

Cauldon

107. Admiral George Dewey, border shows steps in Dewey's career, same design as plate made for a dinner given for Dewey by the Union League Club. $55.

Copeland

108. Buffalo Bill Cody, scalloped gadroon border associated with Copeland. $15.

109. King Edward's Hotel, Toronto, Canada. $45.

110. Orphan's Assylum, Brooklyn, New York, 75th anniversary, rare. $80.

111. Pilgrim Couple sometimes called John Alden and Priscilla. $45.

112. Girl at Flax Wheel, small plate from Colonial Times dinner set. $9.

113. Sugar bowl from same set. $25.

114. John Adams Proposing Washington as President of the United States, one of a set. $30.

115. New Orleans views made for
Coleman Adler, Brulatour Courtyard.

116. Lacy Iron Grillwork. $15.

117. Madame John's Legacy. $15.

118. Pirates Alley. $15.

119. St. Louis Cathedral. $15.

120. Lacy Iron Grille Work, a different series of New Orleans, backstamped Coleman and Adler. $15.

121. Spirit of 'Seventy Six (Yankee Doodle). $25.

122. Backstamp of Crown Ducal Colonial Times dinner set.

123. Washington Bicentennial Memorial Plate, part of a series made in 1932, plate in picture 114 is part of same series. $25.

124. Backstamp of memorial plate.

Davenport

All Davenport examples found are of "Western" views—all have the same border.

125. Allen County Courthouse (Fort Wayne, Indiana). $55.

126. St. Louis views, Compton Hill. $60.

127. Eads Bridge, St. Louis. $75.

128. St. Xaviar's Church, St. Louis. $60.

129. Union Station, St. Louis. $60.

130. Kansas State Capitol. $55.

Doulton

131. Balanced Rock, Garden of the Gods, Colorado, most often found border—used only by Doulton. $70.

132. Bermuda, Sir George Somers Wrecked on the Island. $60.

133. Congressional Library, one of a set of six or 12 Washington Views. 50.

134. Gibson Girl, one of a set of 24, "Mr. Waddles Arrives too Late." $110.

135. Islands from Reservoir Hill, East Liverpool, Ohio, Bowman Import. $70.

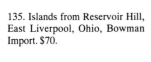

136. Kip-Beekman-Livingston. Hermance House, souvenir of Duchess County Society, New York, 17th annual dinner, rare. $110.

137. Mt. Vernon, old view, before balcony railing and side porch were removed. $70.

138. Tom Turkey, part of a set of
12 plates and a platter. $70.

139. George Washington portrait.
$70.

140. Martha Washington portrait.
$70.

141. White House about 1910.
$70.

142. Grand Canyon National Park, Arizona, ash tray, a cross-collectible wanted by both souvenir and smoking paraphernalia collectors. $10.

143. Grant's Farm, St. Louis, Missouri, type of plate still sold at tourist attractions. $10.

144. Backstamp typical of the 1960s and later.

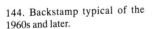

French, Mitchell, and Woodbury

145. Bar Harbor, Maine. $25.

146. Custis Lee Mansion. $40.

147. Governor Langdon House. $40.

148. High Rock Springs, Saratoga, New York. $50.

149. House of the Seven Gables. $50.

150. Illinois Women's College, Jacksonville, Illinois. $40.

151. Morse High School, Bath, Maine. $40.

152. Stewart Haskill Free Library. $35.

153. Soldiers' Monument, Allentown, Pennsylvania. $30.

154. Yankee Doodle. $35.

Greenfield Pottery

155. Boston, contemporary plate. $5.

Harker Pottery

156. Plymouth Rock, porcelain, many examples exist of this type, generally views are of buildings or events of local interest. $10.

Holland tiles

157. Beacon Hill, Boston, signed G.M. Goff, '68. $7.

158. Boston State House. $7.

159. Old Ironsides. $7.

160. Old State House. $7.

161. S.S. Peter Stuyvesant (ship). $7.

Hughes

162. Lookout Mountain, Tennessee, identical to Davenport, same time period. $65.

Johnson Brothers

163. Historic America plate from dinner set. $15.

164. Small dish from Historic America dinner set, these were made in pink and blue. $12.

165. Brochure showing pieces available (with prices) in the Historic America set.

166. Pennsylvania German Folklore Society of Ontario, Canada, 1960. $10.

167. Oregon City. $10.

168. Mt. Rushmore. $5.

169. Jones, McDuffee, and Stratton 100th Anniversary Plate. $110.

170. Back view of anniversary plate, story of firm's activities and history.

171. 1922 calendar tile, Cathedral Church of St. Paul, see Wedgwood section for complete list of calendar tiles. $50.

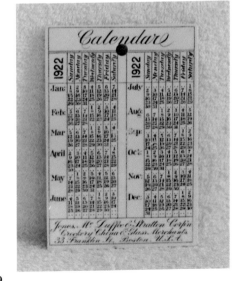

172. Calendar side of tile with Jones, McDuffee, and Stratton logo.

173. Bennington, Vermont, resembles Beardmore and Wheelock designs. $15.

174. Coolidge Home, marked only Jonroth, probably about 1940. $20.

175. Eternal Light, Peace Monument, Gettysburg, resembles rolled edge Rowland and Marsellus, but marked Jonroth. $35.

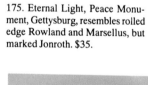

176. Reverse of Peace Monument plate with complete Gettysburg Address.

177. Franconia Notch, New Hampshire, resembles Ye Old Historical Pottery plates, marked Jonroth. $30.

178. Hermitage, Home of Andrew Jackson, marked Jonroth. $20.

179. Pilgrim Memorial Monument, Provincetown, Massachusetts, (late 1940s). $20.

180. Washington, D.C. $15.

181. Edgar Lee Masters. $10.

182. Fulton County, Illinois. $10.

183. Rasmussen Blacksmith Shop Museum (Lewistown, Illinois). $10.

184. Sixteenth President. $7.

185. Photo of booklet issued by company in 1928.

CONCERNING

THE

BLUE CHINA

THE BALTIMORE AND OHIO
RAILROAD COMPANY

DINING CAR DEPARTMENT

The dinner plates, for sale as souvenirs, may be secured from the stewards of dining cars, at $1.00 each.

For information in relation to purchase of any of the other pieces (prices listed below), please communicate with the Manager Dining Car and Commissary Department, Baltimore, Md.

This booklet was prepared originally for the Baltimore and Ohio Centenary Exhibition and Pageant held in 1927, Baltimore, Md., which was known as the "Fair of the Iron Horse".

PRICE LIST

	Price (each)		Price (each)
Bakers—Large	$ .70	Pitcher—2 Qt.	$2.65
Small	.60	12 Oz.	1.35
Medium	.65	Plates—Dinner	1.00
Butter Chips	.20	Tea	.75
Cake Covers	1.10	Soup	1.00
Celery Troughs	2.35	Bread and Butter	.60
Chocolate Pots	2.00		
Compartment Plate	3.00	Platters—Extra large	3.45
Comport	3.15	Large	3.15
Cups—After Dinner	.70	Medium	1.70
Bouillon	.80	Small	1.10
Coffee	.80	Saucers—After Dinner	.30
Egg	.80	Coffee	.50
Gravy Boats	1.40		
Ice Cream Shells	.65	Sauce Dishes	.45
Oatmeal Bowls—Large	.65		
Small	.70	Tea Pots	2.25

186. Photo of page offering pieces for sale.

187. Railroad china lunch plate. $60.

188. Railroad china butter plate. $35.

189. The United States Squadron Before Algiers, porcelain, one of a series, marked Shenango—after 1955. $12.

190. Backstamp of United States Squadron plate gives details of battle.

Homer Laughlin

191. Historical America platter from dinner set. $20.

192. Historical America small plate, Paul Revere's Ride. $10.

Mason's

193. Dominion of Canada, many plates of this type were issued in 1926 or a little later. $20.

194. Niagara Falls. $20.

195. University of Western Ontario Jubilee 1938. $15.

Alfred Meakin

196. Beauvoir House, Jefferson Davis shrine, contemporary plate. $10.

197. Cypress Gardens, 4 1/2 inch plate, contemporary. $4.

J. and G. Meakin

198. Niagara Falls, odd square shape. $20.

205. Santa Barbara, California, Mission. $45.

206. Stenton, same border as Water Works plate, same series? $40.

Pope Gosser

207. Lafayette, Indiana, 100th anniversary, 1925. $50.

208. A. Lincoln, green with blue center, very unusual, paneled border. $40.

209. A. Lincoln, wild roses border. $30.

210. A. Lincoln, paneled border. $30.

211. Illinois State Capitol, wild roses border. $30.

212. Indianapolis, Indiana, Soldiers and Sailors Monument, paneled border. $30.

213. Indianapolis, Indiana, State Capitol, paneled border. $30.

214. Mount Vernon, paneled border, all Regout plates except the Holland Liberation plate date from about 1909. $30.

215. Liberation of Holland, Maastricht, the First Liberated City of Holland, 1944. $25.

Ridgway

216. Beehive Store, where? About 1910. $30.

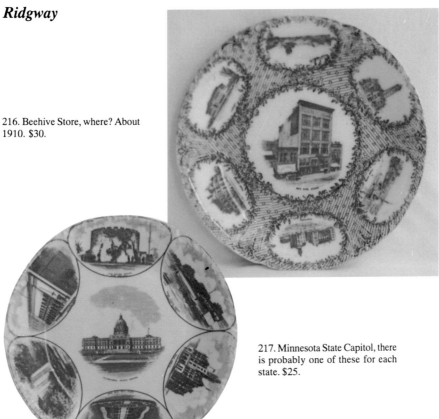

217. Minnesota State Capitol, there is probably one of these for each state. $25.

218. New York City Hall, one of a series. $25.

219. Omaha Auditorium, semi-porcelain. $30.

220. State House, (where?) $25.

221. United States Capitol. $30.

222. Martha Washington portrait. $60.

Rowland and Marsellus

All plates pictured are clearly marked R and M. Unmarked pieces should be regarded with suspicion. The reproductions coming from Taiwan and Japan are obvious to the experienced collector, but the copies are getting better! Some are made of earthenware similar to the old ones.

Fruit and flower border

223. Altoona, Pennsylvania, Horseshoe Curve. $55.

224. Battle of Bunker Hill. $60.

225. Battle of Germantown. $60.

226. Biltmore House. $45.

227. Block House, four sides, no location—could be from 1893 World's Columbian Exposition in Chicago. $50.

228. Block House, six sides—location not given. $50.

229. Bunker Hill Monument. $50.

230. Capitol, Washington, D.C. $50.

231. Clara Barton Birthplace. $60.

232. DeSoto's Discovery of the Mississippi. $65.

233. Ellsworth Homestead. $60.

234. Faneuil Hall. $60.

235. Federal Hall, Wall Street. $60.

236. Hermitage, Home of Andrew Jackson. $60.

237. Home of George and Martha Washington. $55.

238. John Alden and Priscilla. $55.

239. Lowell, Massachusetts, City Hall, unusual, most civic building scenes have a rolled edge border. $50.

240. Minnesota State Capitol, rare. $80.

140

241. Niagara Falls. $65.

242. Old South Church. $60.

243. Plymouth Rock. $60.

244. Ride of Paul Revere. $65.

245. Surrender of Colonel William Ledyard. $65.

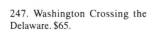

246. Waltham Watch Factory, rare. $80.

247. Washington Crossing the Delaware. $65.

248. Whirlpool Rapids, Niagara Falls. $80.

Coupe shape

249. Alaska-Yukon Exposition, one of several views. $60.

250. American Poets, black. $40.

251. American Poets, blue. $50.

252. Annapolis Basin, Nova Scotia. $50.

253. Golden Gate by Moonlight, San Francisco, California. $45.

Cups and saucers

254. Detroit, Michigan. $65.

255. Lewis and Clark Centennial saucer. $40.

256. Minneapolis, Minnesota. $60.

257. Plymouth, Massachusetts. $65.

258. St. Louis World's Fair, 1904. $85.

259. Photo of Burbank backstamp, circa 1900. The Burbank Store imported numerous items with views of Plymouth and vicinity including postcards and souvenir spoons.

Odds

260. Crawford Cooking Ranges, creamer and platter also made, other firms also imported these items. $60.

261. Discovery of America pitcher, brown. $65.

262. Discovery of America pitcher, green. $75.

263. Harrisburg, Pennsylvania, floral border plate. $35.

264. Montreal, Canada, green, porcelain. $30.

265. Plymouth Pilgrims, pitcher, green. $50.

266. Plymouth Pilgrims, pitcher, blue. $70.

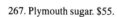

267. Plymouth sugar. $55.

268. Creamer, matches the Plymouth sugar. $55.

269. Plymouth, Canopy over Plymouth Rock, 5 inch flat plate. $40.

270. Plymouth, views of, 6 inches. $40.

271. Plymouth Rock, 5 inches. $45.

272. Plymouth in 1622, platter, rare. $200-$600.

273. Salt Lake City, views of, 5 inches. $35.

275. Washington, D.C., views of, 5 inches. $40.

274. St. Louis, vase from 1904 World's Fair. $150.

276. Yale, coupe shape, five views, 6 1/2 inches. $35.

Rolled edge plates: the rolled edge plates are all 10 inches in diameter, a few were made in odd colors. One should always check the backstamp as other firms also used this style and some new plates are being made with a modified rolled edge.

277. Asbury Park, New Jersey. $50.

278. Baltimore, Indiana, misprint? Border scenes are of the city of Baltimore, Maryland. $70.

279. Boston, historical, Faneuil Hall. $60.

280. Boston, Tremont Street Mall. $65.

281. Buffalo, New York, Library and Soldiers Monument. $75.

282. Butte, Montana, rare. $90.

283. Captain John Smith. $80.

284. Cleveland, Ohio, Garfield Memorial. $70.

285. Grand Rapids, Michigan, City Hall. $65.

286. Home, Sweet Home, John Howard Payne. $70.

287. Kansas City, Missouri, Convention Hall. $70.

288. Lake Champlain, Ausable Chasm. $75.

289. Lewis and Clark Centennial. $90.

290. Longfellow's Home. $65.

291. Los Angeles, Court House. $70.

292. Miles Standish Monument. $65.

293. New St. Peter's Church. $60.

294. Newport, Rhode Island, Old Stone Mill. $70.

295. Niagara Falls. $65.

296. Panama-Pacific International Exposition. $95.

297. Philadelphia City Hall. $70.

298. Philadelphia, Historical. $70.

299. Plymouth Rock. $65.

300. Backstamp of Plymouth Rock plate.

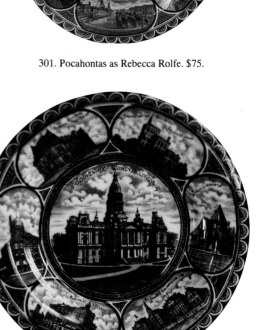

301. Pocahontas as Rebecca Rolfe. $75.

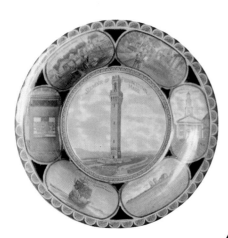

302. Provincetown Massachusetts, strange color combination. $40.

303. Quincy, Illinois, Court House. $60.

304. Richfield Springs, New York. $60.

305. St. Louis Centennial, 1909. $90.

306. Salem, Massachusetts, Witch House. $75.

307. Backstamp of Salem plate.

308. Salt Lake, Temple Square. $70.

309. Spokane, Washington, view of falls. $65.

310. Taft and Sherman, political plate. $85.

311. Teddy Roosevelt portrait. $80.

312. Toronto, Canada. $60.

313. Troy, New York, Emma Willard School. $65.

314. Valley Forge in Summer. $70.

315. Valley Forge in Winter. $70.

316. World's Fair, St. Louis, Thomas Jefferson portrait. $110.

317. Yale, Old Brick Row. $60.

318. Faneuil Hall, Ye Old Historical Pottery, No. 1. $60.

319. Backstamp, there should be some logic to the numbering system, but no one seems to have decoded it as yet.

Royal Staffordshire Pottery

320. Alamo, San Antonio, Texas, cereal bowl, contemporary, but very unusual. $6.

321. Landing of the Pilgrims. $20.

322. Little White House, Warm Springs, Georgia. $15.

323. Moccasin Bend from Lookout Mountain. $10.

324. Salem, Massachusetts, creamer. $10.

325. Salem creamer, different color. $10.

326. Salem, Massachusetts, cup. $10.

327. Andrew Jackson, First governor of Florida, larger than other two examples, part of a different series? $45.

328. Old City Gates, St. Augustine, Florida. $50.

329. Ponce de Leon, portrait. $40.

Syracuse China

330. Community Church, Park Ridge, Illinois. $5.

Vernon Kilns

331. Georgia State Capitol, Atlanta. $10.

332. Indiana, state of. $8.

333. Michigan, state of. $8.

334. Picture Map of North Carolina. $9.

335. Veiled Prophet, St. Louis, year not given, parade no longer held. $10.

336. Williams, Arizona. $7.

Warwick

337. Ohio Canal at Massillon. $30.

Wedgwood

**Not Jones, McDuffee, and
Stratton.**

338. Franconia Notch, Old ramp,
early 1880s. $35.

339. Franconia Notch, Old ramp, later re-issue. $30.

340. Franconia Notch, Old Stone Face, early 1880s. $35.

341. Franconia Notch, Old Stone Face pitcher, pre 1890. $45.

342. Old Town Square, Plymouth, early, pre-1890. $30.

343. Tamsen School, cup and saucer, 1955, issued by the D.A.R. $15.

344. Fort Dearborn, black center, made for World's Columbian Exposition or Dearborn, Michigan? $50.

345. Lynn Club House, tile. $40.

346. Old North Church, tile. $50.

347. World's Columbian Exposition, Agricultural Building. $20.

348. World's Columbian Exposition, Administration Building. $20.

349. Backstamp showing patent rights.

350. Poet series-Longfellow plate. $25.

351. Poet series-Whittier plate. $25.

Wedgwood, Jones, McDuffee, and Stratton, pre-1910

All are 9 1/4 inches in diameter, all are deep blue with cabbage rose borders. Jones, McDuffee, and Stratton also imported other views before 1910. These are in the second group of pictures.

353. Alexandria Bay, New York (courtesy of Dick and Noni Manley). $45.

352. Adjacent Leanto Houses. $40.

354. Benton Harbor, Michigan, The City (courtesy of Dick and Noni Manley). $50.

355. Birth of the American Flag. $40.

356. Block Island, Rhode Island (courtesy of Dick and Noni Manley). $45.

357. Boston in 1776. $40.

358. Boston Commons and Old State House. $40.

359. Boston Tea Party. $45.

360. Boston Town House. $40.

361. Bunker Hill Monument. $45.

362. Campus Martius. $40.

363. Capture of Vincennes. $55.

364. Capitol, the. $40.

365. Catedal DeAqua Scalkentes, Mexico (courtesy of Dick and Noni Manley). $40.

366. Charter Oak, Hartford, Connecticut (courtesy of Dick and Noni Manley). $45.

367. City Hall, Waterville, Maine (courtesy of Dick and Noni Manley). $45.

368. Cleveland, Grover. $50.

369. East Boston Bethel. $45.

370. Faneuil Hall. $40.

371. First Church in Orrville. $50.

372. First Church, Quincy, Massachusetts. $40.

373. Glenwood Campanella. $45.

374. Grace House in the Fields, New Cannan, Connecticut (courtesy of Dick and Noni Manley). $50.

375. Grand Union Hotel. $60.

376. Grant's Tomb, Riverside on the Hudson (courtesy of Dick and Noni Manley). $45.

377. Green Dragon Tavern. $40.

378. Half Moon on the Hudson. $45.

379. Hermitage, the. $45.

380. Home of Caroline Scott Harrison. $40.

381. Home of Mary A. Livermore. $40.

175

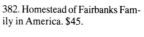
382. Homestead of Fairbanks Family in America. $45.

383. Hoosiac Tunnel, North Adams, Massachusetts (courtesy of Dick and Noni Manley). $50.

384. Hotel Green, Pasadena, California (courtesy of Dick and Noni Manley). $50.

385. Hotel Raymond, Pasadena, California (courtesy of Dick and Noni Manley). $50.

386. House of the Seven Gables. $45.

387. Independence Hall. $45.

388. Interior of Christ Church, Philadelphia, Pennsylvania (courtesy of Dick and Noni Manley). $50.

389. King's Chapel, Boston. $40.

390. Lamb Tavern. $40.

391. Lincoln Home, Springfield, Illinois. $45.

392. Lincoln Monument, Springfield, Illinois. $45.

393. Lockport, New York, 1909 (courtesy of Dick and Noni Manley). $50.

394. Longfellow's Early Home. $40.

395. Longfellow's Home. $40.

396. Maryland Hotel, Pasadena, California (courtesy of Dick and Noni Manley). $50.

397. Massachusetts General Hospital (courtesy of Dick and Noni Manley). $45.

398. Mayflower Arriving in Provincetown. $45.

399. Mayflower in Plymouth Harbor. $45.

400. McKinley Home. $45.

401. McKinley Monument, Buffalo, New York (courtesy of Dick and Noni Manley). $45.

402. Media Hotel and Mineral Baths, Mt. Clemens, Michigan (courtesy of Dick and Noni Manley). $50.

403. Memorial Continental Hall, Washington, D.C., built in 1905. $45.

404. Minnehaha Falls, Minneapolis, Minnesota (courtesy of Dick and Noni Manley). $50.

405. Mt. Vernon. $40.

406. Nathaniel Hawthorne. $50.

407. Old Boston Theatre. $40.

408. Old Brick Church. $40.

409. Old Capitol Building, Albany, New York.

410. Old Man of the Mountain, New Hampshire—distant view (courtesy of Dick and Noni Manley). $50.

411. Old North Bridge. $45.

412. Old North Church. $40.

413. Old South Church. $40.

414. Old State House, Boston. $40.

415. Old Stone Mill, Newport, Rhode Island. $45.

416. Old Town Mill, New London, Connecticut (courtesy of Dick and Noni Manley). $45.

417. Old Windmill, Nantucket, Connecticut (courtesy of Dick and Noni Manley). $50.

418. Onota Lake—Graylock in the Distance (courtesy of Dick and Noni Manley). $60.

419. Orr Docks, Escanaba, Michigan (courtesy of Dick and Noni Manley). $50.

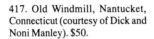

184

420. Park Street Church, Boston. $40.

421. Paul Revere's Ride (courtesy of Dick and Noni Manley). $50.

422. Picturesque Santa Barbara, Hotel Potter (courtesy of Dick and Noni Manley), (only known instance of Wedgwood using the term "picturesque"). $60.

423. Pilgrim Exiles. $45.

424. Backstamp, many Wedgwood plates have historical data on the reverse.

425. Pilgrim Memorial Monument. $45.

426. Poe Lock, Sault Ste, Marie, Michigan (courtesy of Dick and Noni Manley). $50.

427. Priscilla and John Alden. $45.

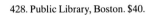
428. Public Library, Boston. $40.

429. Red Lion Inn-in the Berkshires, Stockbridge, Massachusetts, (courtesy of Dick and Noni Manley). $50.

430. Return of the Mayflower. $45.

431. St. Anne by the Sea, Kennebunkport, Maine (courtesy of Dick and Noni Manley). $45.

432. St. Augustine, Old City Gateway. $50.

433. San Carlos DeMonterey or Carmel Mission (courtesy of Dick and Noni Manley). $50.

434. San Fernando Mission, Los Angeles County, California (courtesy of Dick and Noni Manley). $50.

435. San Gabriel Archangel Mission-with bells, (courtesy of Dick and Noni Manley). $50.

436. San Gabriel Archangel Mission-without bells (courtesy of Dick and Noni Manley). $50.

437. San Juan Capistrano (courtesy of Dick and Noni Manley). $50.

438. San Luis Rey, DeFrancia Mission (courtesy of Dick and Noni Manley). $50.

439. Santa Barbara Mission. $55.

440. Saratoga Battle Monument. $45.

441. Signing of the Declaration of Independence. $40.

442. Springfield, Illinois, Capitol Building. $50.

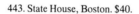

443. State House, Boston. $40.

444. State House and Old State Street, Boston. $40.

445. Summit House, Mt. Tom, New Hampshire (courtesy of Dick and Noni Manley). $45.

446. Summit House, Mt. Tom, New Hampshire-Before the Fire (courtesy of Dick and Noni Manley). $50.

447. Teddy Roosevelt. $60.

448. Trinity Church, Boston. $45.

449. Ulysses S. Grant (courtesy of Dick and Noni Manley). $50.

450. Washington Elm. $45.

451. Washington Monument. $45.

452. Washington, George (portrait). $45.

453. Wayside Inn. $45.

454. White House. $40.

455. Yale College. $40.

456. Champlain Memorial, 1918. $40.

457. Fort Johnson. $35.

458. Fort Ticonderoga Bicentennial, 1955. $20.

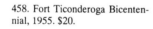

459. Fort Ticonderoga on Lake Champlain. $30.

460. Fort Ticonderoga, South Wall and Barracks. $20.

461. Fort Ticonderoga, Winter Scenes. $20.

462. Harrison Mansion, Vincennes, Indiana, 1928. $35.

463. Home of Cornet Joseph Parsons, ferrara border. $35.

464. Marietta College, Erwin Hall. $20.

465. Old Fauntleroy Home, 1928. $35.

466. Old First Congregational Church, Chicago. $40.

467. Old State House, Boston. $35.

196

468. Longfellow Series, Evangeline. $35.

469. Plumb's Maplewood Hotel. $40.

470. Schofield House, Indiana's Masonic Shrine, Madison, Indiana. $20.

471. State House, Boston. $30.

197

472. World War I Memorial, Augusta, Maine. $35.

473. Old Meeting House, Hingham, Massachusetts, imported by Norcross, Mellen, 1896. $40.

474. Sankoty Lighthouse, ferrara border. $40.

475. Protestant Dutch Church, ferrara border, (imported by Van Heusen, Charles, and Company). $40.

476. Schyler Residence, ferrara border, (imported by Van Heusen, Charles, and Company). $40.

477. Vanderheyden Mansion, ferrara border, (imported by Van Heusen, Charles, and Company). $40.

478. Kent State University, Administration Building. $20.

479. College of the Holy Cross, Alumni Hall. $20.

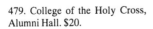

480. Faneuil Hall, bluebell border, 1929. $40.

481. Old North Church, bluebell border, 1930. $40.

482. Illinois College, Jacksonville, Illinois, 1954. $20.

483. Scribner House, New Albany, Indiana. $20.

484. Framingham Academy Library, 1900. $40.

485. Pilgrim Memorial Monument, 1930. $30.

486. Abbot Academy Centennial, 1929. $25.

487. Bennington Battle Monument, 1947. $30.

488. Manchester in the Mountains, 1905. $35.

489. Longfellow's House, after 1907. $40.

490. Railway Post Office Clerks Convention, 1904. $55.

491. Muldoon, Massachusetts, 1899. $55.

492. A. Lincoln statue, embossed border. $45.

493. A. Lincoln statue, smooth border. $40.

494. Waltham Watch Factory. $55.

495. Waltham backstamp, piece could have been part of a lunch service for the cafeteria or dining room of the factory.

496. St. Louis University, 1968. $15.

497. William Henry Harrison Centennial (pink). $15.

498. University of Michigan, 1928, Women's League Building. $20.

499. Washington Bicentennial Plates, Independence Hall, 1932. $20.

500. Webb House, Wethersfield Office. $15.

West Co. Kilns

501. Alaska. $5.

Wheelock

502. Arch Rock, Mackinack Island. $40.

503. Canton, Illinois. $15.

504. Crescent Hotel. $40.

505. Colorado State Capitol. $25.

506. Heart Islands, 1,000 Islands. $40.

507. Hot Springs, Arkansas. $40.

508. Iowa State Capitol. $40.

509. Lexington Park, Lexington, Massachusetts. $15.

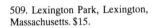

510. Lincoln Home. $30.

511. St. Louis World's Fair 1904. $75.

512. Wichita, Kansas. $15.

Wilkenson, Arthur

513. U.S. Capitol, vegetable bowl. $50.

514. Side view, is this bowl part of a dinner set?

515. Cortland New York State Normal School. $35.

516. Backstamp showing mislabeling, Togo is a pattern name for a dinner set.

517. Denver, Colorado, City Park, many similar plates were made for other Western cities. $30.

518. Gettysburg, Meade, etc. $40.

519. Harrisburg, Pennsylvania, Capitol. $40.

520. Hot Springs, Arkansas. $45. (See photo 507)

521. Newark, New Jersey, department store. $30.

522. Oakland, California, Taft and Kennoyer Building. $30.

523. Richfield Springs, Main Street Bridge. $35.

524. Seattle, Totem Pole. $35.

Wood and Sons

525. Evangelical Congregational
Church, Hingham, Massachusetts.
$10.

526. Constellation, Newport,
Rhode Island. $7.

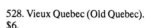

527. Niagara Falls. $10.

528. Vieux Quebec (Old Quebec).
$6.

212

England

(England is the only mark appearing on these pieces — 529-550.)

529. Capitol. $25.

530. Backstamp initials could not be found in Godden.

531. Chain of States—copied from a dinner set given to Martha Washington. $65.

532. Charlestown, West Virginia. $35.

533. Cincinnati, Ohio, Post Office and Gilstom House. $35.

534. Denver, Colorado, State Capitol. $30.

535. Detroit, Michigan, entrance to Detroit River Tunnel. $35.

536. Fort Wayne, Indiana, City Hall. $30.

537. Harrisburg, Pennsylvania State Capitol. $35.

538. Muskogee, Oklahoma. $15.

539. Lincoln, Nebraska. $15.

540. Kansas City, Missouri. $30.

541. Keokuk, Iowa. $30.

542. Minneapolis, Minnesota. $30.

543. Mt. Tom. $15.

544. Portland, Maine. $15.

545. Salem Reform Church, Allentown, Pennsylvania. $30.

546. White Plains, New York, platter, made for the D.A.R. $85.

547. Salt Lake City, Utah. $35.

548. St. Louis, Missouri, Court House and Modern St.Louis, Missouri. $35.

549. Seattle, Washington, Carnegie Library. $30.

217

550. Yellowstone National Park, Old Faithful, new. $5.

Unmarked

551. Bangor, Maine pier. $15.

552. Cardiff Castle. $25.

553. Court of Ferdinand and Isabella, American made, part of a lunch set? $5.

554. Duluth, Minnesota. $35.

555. Evangeline. $45.

556. Faneuil Hall. $35.

557. Home of Franklin Roosevelt. $5.

558. Old Stone Mill, Newport, Rhode Island. $8.

559. Pennsylvania Society of New York. $45.

560. Primitive Methodist Church Centenary. $35.

561. Quincy, Massachusetts. $20.

562. University of Notre Dame. $5.

563. William Shakespeare. $25.

564. Reproduction, Hannibal, Missouri, not marked, probably made in Japan or Taiwan. $4.

221

Index

BIBLIOGRAPHY

Antiques Journal, 1950-1980

Barber, Edwin Atlee. *Marks of American Potters.* Southhampton, New York: Cracker Barrel Press, n.d.

Burgess, Arene W. *Souvenir Plates: A Collector's Guide.* Bethalto, Illinois, 1978.

Godden, G.A. *Encyclopaedia of British Pottery and Porcelain Marks.* New York: Crown, 1964

Hobbies, 1950-1980

Jackson, Mary, L. *If Dishes Could Talk.* Des Moines, Iowa: Wallace Homestead Book Company, 1971

Kamm, Minnie Watson. *Old China.* Grosse Pointe, Michigan: Kamm Publications, 1951

Laidacker, Sam. *Anglo-American China (Parts I and II).* Bristol, Pennsylvania: Sam Laidacker, 1954

Lehner, Lois. *U.S. Marks on Pottery, Porcelain and Clay.* Paducah, Kentucky: Collector Books, 1988

Spinning Wheel, 1950-1980

Stefano, Frank, Jr. *Pictorial Souvenirs and Commemoratives of North America.* New York: E.P. Dutton and Company, 1976

Stefano, Frank, Jr. *Check List of Wedgwood Old Blue Historical Plates and Other Views of the United States.* Produced for Jones, McDuffee and Stratton, privately printed, July 1971

Williams, Petra. *Flow Blue China, an Aid to Identification.* Jeffersontown, Kentucky: Fountain House East, 1971

Williams, Petra. *Flow Blue China II.* Jeffersontown, Kentucky: Fountain House East, 1973

Williams, Petra. *Flow Blue China and Mulberry Ware.* Jeffersontown, Kentucky: Fountain House East, 1975